BUILDING IN THE STORM

COLIN SCOTT

Building in the Storm

Copyright © 2025 Colin Scott

First edition published 2025.

The moral right of the author to full ownership of the copyright of *'Building in the Storm'* has been asserted. All rights are reserved. The book may not be reproduced in part or whole without prior written permission from the publisher. However, extracts for the purpose of Bible study, sermons, and reviews in magazines, newspapers, radio and television, and short quotations in other books are allowed.
No part of this book may be used or reproduced in any manner for the purpose of training artificial intelligence technologies, systems or any future technology.

Scripture references marked (NKJV) are from the New King James Version. Copyright © 1982 by Thomas Nelson, Inc. Used by permission. All rights reserved.

Cover Art and Design by: Kyra Matla (with help of AI)

Fonts used for content – Tinos

Copies of *Building in the Storm* are available in New Zealand to be purchased direct from the author who can be contacted at colinmscott01@gmail.com.

Published in New Zealand

A catalogue record for this book is available
from the National Library of New Zealand.

Paperback ISBN: 978-0-473-74048-1

BUILDING IN THE STORM

COLIN SCOTT

Acknowledgements

It goes without saying, that I give as much credit for the revelations I have put in this book to our creator God. That's exactly how I view them, life-giving knowledge that has been revealed to me. Faith comes by hearing, but it is dead until you give life to it by letting it shape how you live. Thank you, Lord, for giving life to me while resisting this storm.

I am one of those who in my hunger for life-giving revelation, have heaped up teachers. For the most part though, I have been relying on the Holy Spirit to teach me through whoever is speaking. So really, I only have one teacher.

I do want to specifically acknowledge three teachers who have been used to shape my thinking more than others, and that is Curry Blake, Dan Mohler, and Andrew Womack. While many believe Romans 8:28 means God will do whatever He wants to make things good, I believe He is saying He will work with those who are willing to bring good out of anything.

These three guys I see as willing to work with God to bring people a more abundant life. This is the call we all have, to walk with God, not just visit Him on a Sunday when we don't have something better on.

I want to specifically acknowledge my friend John Kinghorn. He has and continues to stir me to faith, and to keep my eyes above and not below. I would love everyone to have a brother like him.

Lastly, I am so grateful for my wife. I have truly found a good thing. She continues to love and support me despite the challenges I present her at times. My children are blessed to call her mum.

Contents

- INTRODUCTION 7
- RUN THE RACE 11
- BIBLE-BELIEVING 21
  - Pressing on 24
- SOVEREIGN SAVIOUR 33
  - Second Half 44
- CHOICE, NOT FREE WILL 49
  - Sowing 57
- SUBMIT, NOT SURRENDER 65
  - Replacement 70
- RESIST, REST, REPEAT 75
  - Rest 87
- FAITH, NOT FATE 97
- HOPE VS WISHING 107
- LOVE AND HATE 117
- ANOINTING AND AUTHORITY 127
  - Authority 135
- PURSUING PEACE 145
  - The Feeling 153
- TEMPTATIONS, TRIALS, AND TESTS 159
- SICKNESS OR SUFFERING? 169
  - Revelation 173
- HEALING HYPE 183

Introduction

I had a revelation recently that it's not my responsibility to make others believe right. Jesus can take care of that with them. The commandment for me is to love people, not to convince them to agree with my reasoning.

This does not mean I am not pursuing truth, to be sanctified in it, and to grow in the freedom it brings. But my desire is to walk more closely with God, and to seek life and peace – not on trying to be right.

> *For God did not send His Son into the world to condemn the world, but that the world through Him might be saved.*
>
> *John 3:17*

It was not Jesus's purpose to point out our failing to 'meet right', but that through Him we might be saved, and as John 10:10 says, have life. In this book, I share what I believe, but my goal is not to convince you to believe as I do, but that I may build you up, stir you to faith, and help you toward a more abundant life.

What is building in the storm?

> *"Therefore, whoever hears these sayings of Mine, and does them, I will liken him to a wise man who built his house on the rock:*
>
> *Matthew 7:24*

It may come as a surprise, but this verse does not say, "Whoever is redeemed, will build their house wisely." People can be saved, and still not build well.

The storm that descended upon me in the form of health challenges exposed how foolishly I had built. But rather than just sit in the rubble of my collapsed house, I'm working with our merciful Saviour to build a new one. I'm <u>building in the storm</u>. My hope in writing these words is that I may help others build houses that stand in any weather, and before a storm comes.

> *According to the grace of God which was given to me, as a wise master builder I have laid the foundation, and another builds on it. But let each one take heed how he builds on it.*
>
> *1 Corinthians 3:10*

I am not labelling myself a master builder, just highlighting our necessity to take heed. I include many Scripture references in this writing, because we stand on His Word, not on mine.

In this book, I ask many questions, not because I don't know what I believe, but for you to consider what you do. A powerful way God answers my questions, is often with a better question. This is how Jesus frequently responded. A key role of Holy Spirit is to lead us into all truth. I hope to pose questions Holy Spirit can use to guide you.

Run the Race

Imagine finding yourself at the starting line of a race. A large crowd has gathered to cheer you on. The entry fee has been paid, which was surprisingly high for a race. All set and ready for the go, it starts dawning on you, "I don't even know what this race is!" Is it a sprint, a marathon, an orienteering course? You grab a copy of the rule book and skim through it hoping to find something helpful, but before you can get the gist of it, BANG! the gun fires. You set off running, looking to see what others will do.

Some seem unsure, while others don't appear concerned they are in a race. A few look like they know what they are doing – like they may have done some training – so you join with the group following them. After a while, you notice they are not following the rules you remember seeing in the rule book. Many seem to be doing the same though, so maybe it's okay.

Should you copy them? Does it even matter?

What would cause you to find out the real purpose of the race and what the rules actually are? The fee was just so big. Jesus didn't only lay down His spare change so you could compete, He laid down His life. The Bible tells us a great cloud of witnesses is watching us. Even angels seem to care what we do. It might be easy or comfortable to follow the crowd, to keep running as we are, but what is the cost if we do? The way that *seems* right leads to death (Proverbs 14:12), which is a price I don't want to pay.

We are warned not to lean on our understanding (sight; seeing what others do), that wide is the way (common; accepted by the majority) that leads to destruction. Do I really want to just follow others? A quick internet search shows an estimated more than 2.3 billion people in the world today who label themselves as Christian. Is that what you would call 'wide?'

> *Therefore we also, since we are surrounded by so great a cloud of witnesses, let us lay aside every weight, and the sin which so easily ensnares us, and let us run with endurance the race that is set before us...*
>
> *Hebrews 12:1*

If you were serious about running a race well in the physical, you would find out a couple of things first. Like, what type of race it is, rules to be aware of, the prize if you place. When you know these things, you can prepare much better than if you found out on the day. If the race was a marathon, you would train differently than you would for a sprint. You may buy different gear if you were entering a cross-country up a snowy mountain. Do you need to know how to use a compass? If the prize was worth winning, you might choose to be more disciplined in your lifestyle. The more you want to win, the bigger priority it is not to be hindered.

In the race set before us there are two things that make it harder to run – weight and sin. I see sin similar to having a nap under a tree (like the tortoise and hare story), making something else more important than running. You could wake up to find you have been asleep for hours. It may seem harmless at the time, but it can make a big mess of your race.

Without a desire to win the race (vision), people perish

This book is not about listing sins to avoid. I am not going to judge your faults and attempt to make you miserable as you run. But I will certainly encourage you to go and sin no more. From my experience, the more you want to run well, the less opportunity you give to distractions (2 Timothy 2:4). I want to focus our attention on the idea of *weight*.

Weight to me describes things that make it harder to run, like having your legs tied together. We may find weight in various things like taking care of family matters, inspecting our oxen (work), spending time as newlyweds, etc., but I have come to realise the more important weight to address is unbelief, or perverse thinking (wrong belief). Although you might not consider believing as something you are carrying – like running with a child in your arms – I picture it as trying to reach our destination with an upside down map.

I would rather cross the finish line panting from carrying too much, than end up in the middle of nowhere wondering where I went wrong.

What is the race and is it worth running well?

I very strongly encourage you to answer this question. If you don't, you will likely find yourself living according to sight by default, and not by belief (faith) on purpose.

There are many opinions about this, but what does God say? What is said by the One who actually set the race before you? At the end of the day, you don't have to answer to me, or even yourself, feelings, parents, friends, pastors, church, or anyone else. Who is going to question the way you ran? What are the plans God has for you (Jeremiah 29:11), or the good works He has for you to walk in (Ephesians 2:10)? If you believe you are called according to His purpose, what is *His* purpose (Romans 8:28)?

Personally, I believe the race is a combination of loving God, loving people, and renewing my mind to understand who I am in Christ. There are many things we are instructed in the Bible, but I find that most of them fit well under these three categories. I don't think it is good for us to be so focussed on renewing our minds, trying to grasp being more 'like God', that we are not obedient to what He has already commanded us to do, being hearers only. At the same time, we shouldn't be so focussed on doing good, that we do not walk with Him.

Depending on what you think the prize is, and your desire to win it, will determine the effort you put in to attain it. The minimum reward, like a participation certificate, would be doing just enough to secure a place in heaven. This does not require much effort. Just receive it, no works demanded. You only have to fall across the starting line. You could be nailed to a cross next to Jesus, unable to do a single thing but repent, and you would still be with Him in paradise. If you need to pay any price for it, then it is not a free gift.

His grace is by far the best good news there is

The maximum prize, however, may be far beyond what you could think or imagine. John 14:12 says *if* you believe in me, you will do the works that I (Jesus) do. Are you doing them? Could you? Is the way you are believing causing you to pay the price of not being able to do them?

Scripture tells us that nothing is impossible to him who believes (Matthew 17:20, Mark 9:23). If you cannot 'cast it out' like the disciples, is that because it was not possible? Or was it in fact available had you been running differently? Is the way you are running putting a limit on what you can do? How much power is working in you (Ephesians 3:20)? We know and quote that the same power that rose Christ from the dead lives in us, but do we run in such a way that allows that power to work?

Paul says we should run in such a way that we may obtain the prize (1 Corinthians 9:24), but what do you think the prize is? I hope this question will grab many! There is a way to run. He said he had run his race (2 Timothy 4:7), and also said he didn't claim to apprehend (Philippians 3:13). I do not think we can say we are running our race perfectly, but we could be pressing and reaching, going from glory to glory until we cross the earthly finish line.

Does the race have any rules?

Imagine turning up to the starting line to discover it was a cycle race, but your bike was at home and you couldn't compete. We can be as fit as we want, as good a person as we can manage, but without Jesus we are disqualified. If you don't know Him, decide if you want to, then ask Him to reveal Himself to you. Jesus loves you so much more than you realise. Give Him an opportunity to show you.

What if the race required doing things along the way, e.g. a scavenger hunt, and not just crossing the finish line. If we want to run the race ahead of us well, we must know the rules and compete accordingly, especially if we are wanting to run as one who will win (2 Timothy 2:5).

> *Do you not know that those who run in a race all run, but one receives the prize? Run in such a way that you may obtain it.*
>
> *1 Corinthians 9:24*

Are there instructions God wants us to follow? There are, but until we acknowledge they matter, we will not live by them. As an example, 'If you remain in me, you will bear much fruit'. (John 15:5) What are the instructions? It is not to pray for fruit, but to remain in Him. Hebrews 6:12 says to imitate those who through faith and patience inherit the promises. Are you wanting to receive something? What are the instructions? Faith and patience, or praying and begging? Are you wanting peace? Isaiah 26:3 says, 'You will keep him in perfect peace whose mind is stayed on You, because he trusts in You.' Although God in His mercy might gift things to people at times, there are ways He would prefer you lived by.

Is there anything else our Father has put in place for us to follow? How about prayer, fasting, abiding, faith, sowing and reaping, discipline, holiness, humility and perseverance, etc.? Moving away briefly from the running analogy, it is like knowing what fertiliser you need to apply to the seed (God's Word) to reap the best harvest. Some thirty-, some sixty-, some one hundred-fold. What should you use to get the best yield? Light, dark, warm, cold, wet, dry? If you don't know what makes the plant grow, you may prevent it from flourishing.

Knowing how to run is very important. We can spend (waste) a lot of time doing things our way, following the reasoning of experience (sight), or we can read the Word and ask the Author and Finisher of our faith to show us. The easiest way for me to understand this, is knowing whether we are supposed to be kicking the ball under or over the post. I am not sure why people would kick the ball and then ask God to determine where it lands, if they have already been told. If we know, we should be aiming for that, pressing and reaching, and praying for His help to hit the mark.

Is there a better way to run?

My story is that I spent a long time running in no particular direction. I had crossed the starting line and secured my participation award, but I wasn't running according to any rules. Due to being tripped over (by health challenges), I looked up and realised that I was far behind where I wanted to be, and that my running needed to change.

I stopped following the way that seemed right and got out the rule book (His Word). I started following what it said instead of following others, and very quickly found a new stride that took me far ahead of where I was. My new running style gave me such an improved outlook on the race. I'm sharing some of my insights here in the hope it may encourage and assist others in their running, and if some find themselves tripped over (falling into various trials), that it will help them pick themselves up.

Just imagine for half a second Jesus asking you for an account of what he had given His life for (the entry fee). Was it only so you could get to heaven – Christ in you? Or was it for more – the hope of glory, glory being Him seen and known. Not the guarantee of glory but the hope of it. If I see you, can I see the Father? Or is your light being covered by unbelief? Christ in you should look like something the world wants (Acts 8:18-19) and cause them to ask about the hope in you – Christ, our living hope.

We should take heed how we build on the foundation laid, which is Jesus Christ. The way we run – our faith, our works, the things we have done – will be tested by fire (1 Corinthians 3:10-15). Are you confident that you are doing what He is looking for?

By grace we have been saved (Ephesians 2:8), not by works (Ephesians 2:9), but that doesn't mean there are no works He has planned for you (Ephesians 2:10). Do you desire to run the race He wants, His way, the one He set before you? Or do you think He should just be happy with the way you are running? Should He allow you to break His rules and still get the same treasure and reward of someone who runs according to them? He can do what He wants (Matthew 20:15). But He is a just God.

What weight is hindering Christians (believers)?

This is the question in the back of my mind as I write what follows.

As I learned how to run better, I saw an immediate increase of heaven on earth. I'm not saying that I have all the answers, but there are things I found in the Bible and in prayer I want to share with you. These changes in my believing have made a big difference in my life.

Bible-Believing

As we press into the following revelations, I feel very strongly to remind people that God is merciful. We really need to understand who He is before we discuss our part to play.

We can allow ourselves to fall into the trap of trying to do things just in our own strength – works, formulas, or methods we think should get the results we want. There is the way God wants us to run our race, but we must not forget that we are in a covenant, partnership, friendship, sonship with Him. We must not be ignorant that there can be a cost when we do not choose life, i.e. when we give place to the devil, fail to sow, do not renew our minds, etc., but we must have hope in His mercy and grace. If you lose sight of the Cross, the weight of trying to attain your own righteousness will crush you.

There are many Scriptures about us winning in partnership with Him, but one of my favourites is…

And they overcame him by the blood of the Lamb and by the word of their testimony, and they did not love their lives to the death.

Revelation 12:11

We overcome with His part *and* our part. Some people will try to do life only relying on their strength, but we won because Jesus went to the cross!

People at times use their life experiences, or even passages in the Bible, to reason who God is. <u>*He is who He says He is!*</u> We need to stop trying to put God within the limits of our thinking, leaning on our own understanding. We need to trust Him, not redefine Him (Proverbs 3:5-6). We are told many times in the Word that He is merciful and compassionate – so He *is*, regardless of how our life plays out. It's the Word that describes Him, not our experience.

His grace is sufficient. He is strong when we are weak. He is faithful. Both Jesus and Holy Spirit intercede for us. Jesus gives rest to those who come to Him. Holy Spirit is our Helper and Comforter.

Read Romans 8:26, 31-39 for encouragement.

God is for you!

This book may be challenging at times, as it directly confronts our believing. I am writing to stir you to faith, not lull you to sleep. I hope to convict you, not to condemn you. I tackle the way we see God, ourselves, and the view that we can still have the fruit of being in the vine without taking responsibility to live connected to it.

> *For judgment is without mercy to the one who has shown no mercy. Mercy triumphs over judgment.*
>
> *James 2:13*

*Father, thank you for your mercies.
Help me to believe the truth (sanctify me),
to act justly, and teach me to love mercy
as I walk trusting you.*

(Inspired from Micah 6:8, Proverbs 3:5-6 and John 17:17)

Pressing on

With that said and prayed, have you ever not had something go the way you hoped? What if it could have? Is there a price you would be willing to pay for things to go differently?

Some people say that they wouldn't change a thing about their past, that it made them who they are, but there is some stuff in my past I would definitely change if I could. There is a great deal of sin I would not commit, people I would not hurt or disappoint, things I would not have spent time on, and people who I would have ministered life (the Kingdom) to. More importantly, I would have made it a bigger priority to strengthen my relationship with my Father in heaven and my connection to the Vine. However, spending time imagining the could-have-beens will, unfortunately, not change what was.

Paul of Tarsus, who had a rather bad past, gave us some much-needed advice on how to deal with this. In Philippians 3:13-14, he said, '…forgetting those things which are behind and reaching forward for those things which are ahead…'. We can get so caught up in looking backwards that we do not choose to change our gaze and look forward. This does not mean having wilful amnesia or creating black spots in our memory. It simply means we do not let how the past went determine how the future goes.

Regardless of how bad our past may have been, we need to give it to God. We thank Him that we are not condemned, neither do we hold any unforgiveness, and we know that He is in the business of working things out for good. We must do this intentionally, throwing off all that hinders us – all the wrong done by us (not denying responsibility for our actions, but not taking guilt that makes us inwardly focussed) and all the wrong done to us.

According to the Word, wrong believing can lead to death and destruction (Proverbs 14:12, Hosea 4:6). Alternatively, if we believe correctly, Jesus said that all things are possible (Mark 9:23). The definition of all used in that verse is *all*, and the word 'possible' is the same word used in Matthew 19:26 where it says all things are possible with God. If you are not believing it is possible for you, are you putting a limit on God? Likewise, if you know it's not possible for God, i.e. it involves lying, stealing, something unjust or unloving, then you probably shouldn't be trying to believe for it.

Either you are not concerned by this and continue to think 'what will be will be', or you need to answer the following question…

What is right believing?

In my own walk with God, I had determined what I would believe based on how my life was going. I leant on my understanding and the way that seemed right to me. I accepted every experience as if it was the only one available and as the one God wanted for me. I then ignorantly (not knowing better) reasoned out what I went through, and passed that on to others to show how they should approach life. Other people in turn reasoned out their experiences, and I chose to let their understanding guide me. Are we making the Word of God powerless by our passed-on reasoning?

Mark 7:13 says we can do just that!

Often people will look in Scripture for things that agree with what they want to believe, or to try and make sense of how things went for them. As an example, if someone doesn't get healed or fails to minister biblical healing, they look for verses in the Bible they think justify what happened. Would Jesus have had the same result? People will look for variableness in Him when the Word says there is none (James 1:16-17). He healed all who came to Him.

Something else that has become quite noticeable to me recently is how people living in the New Covenant will often use the way God interacted with people in the Old Covenant to explain their life. I know that's a big statement to gloss over, but simply, just like new wine and old wineskins or an unshrunk cloth on an old garment, the two don't mix. Just because you can't understand what is going on, does not give you permission to blend the covenants (Matthew 9:16-17).

People try to reason their experience, before they question if it was the right one

---

What if, by the renewing of our mind, our future did not look like our past? Read Mark 9:14-29 describing the disciples failing to cast out a spirit. Jesus said things would have gone differently if their believing was right (accurate). If Jesus had not shown up, could the disciples have concluded that God doesn't always heal people based on their experience? Imagine if Jesus gave any other reason for their failure besides you faithless (unbelieving) and perverse (wrong-believing) generation (Matthew 17:17-20). Jesus got it done.

Side note: I will talk on this subject later, but I want to say for now that prayer increases our believing and strengthens our faith; not just a way to help us obtain approval or permission.

There are many who would argue that they believe the truth based on their experiences, good or bad. They may say they encounter the power of God more often if they are fasting. Is that truth? I have had a good friend say that they were hearing a voice and believed it was God speaking to them, which they could have taken as truth. Then they were alerted to the fact it wasn't Him, that it was a stranger's voice, and very thankfully did not follow it. I have had an increase in the number of people I see healed. Does my experience indicate I believe the truth?

The devil masquerades as an angel of light and twists (perverts) the truth. What he says will only *seem* right. How do you know it is really God's voice? To not follow the stranger's voice means it can be heard. My sheep know My voice, which means we know when it is not His voice. Don't allow the deceiver any opportunity (resist); make it a priority to know His voice.

Put on the belt of truth

God may tell you whether to buy a house, or marry a certain someone, but do you have a close enough relationship with Him to know it's His voice? We learn how He speaks by spending time getting to know Him (remaining).

People want to believe certain things; I know I did. We can send ourselves to hell by choosing to believe whatever makes us feel comfortable, or by avoiding the light (John 3:20). Some people believe that if there was a God, He would let them into heaven based on their, or His, goodness. What if it only mattered whether they had received Jesus's redemption? Not believing the right thing about that could have eternal consequences. I'm very glad that salvation belongs to the Lord.

> *Woe to those who call evil good, and good evil; Who put darkness for light, and light for darkness; Who put bitter for sweet, and sweet for bitter!*
>
> Isaiah 5:20

Are there things in your past that you have blamed God for, which He had nothing to do with? The enemy would love you to be deceived into calling evil good. We want to infer that things had a purpose or were part of a plan, but in reality, your life may have just been unnecessarily hard at times because of the way you or someone else believed. Leaning on the wrong thing and basing your understanding on that can have costs you don't want to pay.

Could life be influenced by how we believe?

Yes!

The challenge we face is, how do we determine what to believe? What is truth? Is there truth? Am I believing truth, or just someone's reasoning of their experience (*my* truth)? What makes something truth?

Your word is truth! John 17:17

My main point of this chapter is that our reasoning is not truth, God's Word is. At the end of the day, I stand on His Word, not my reasoning.

The truth is God's Word. Jesus is the Truth. God's Word reveals what to believe, Jesus shows me how it is lived out, and gives it flesh. We are to know His Word, His will, and pray it be done, not just let whatever happens be given the place of truth in our lives.

If our experiences are not the same as Jesus would have, then there is more for us to press and reach into. One of the requests I frequently bring to God is, "Sanctify me in the truth."

We must not lean on our own understanding (reasoning of our experience) to tell us what the truth is. We walk by faith (belief) not by sight (experience) as found in 2 Corinthians 5:7. Some truths are black and white, like needing to receive Christ's redemption. Other truths are not so obvious, like knowing the cost of ministering healing, but that does not mean it is not written.

I can confidently say that I believe the truth, because I believe God's Word. I don't claim to apprehend all of it, but I press and reach for my mind to be renewed to it, to be sanctified in the truth.

> # I know His Word is truth, regardless of whether I can understand it

What would it take you?

For me, it was a brain tumour. Do you desire to stop death and destruction in your own life and the lives of others by believing correctly? Or will you continue to walk in your reasoning, wait until the last minute, and then beg God, blaming Him for the outcome?

Our God determined seed time and harvest in the natural and in the spiritual. This means the fruit of our believing grows. His words are seeds that grow into trees that bear fruit.

> # We need to stop trying to meet needs with seeds when people are hungry for fruit

Whether you have fruit ready or not, in season or out, does not determine the truth that was in the seed. God's Word is true regardless of the time you planted it, the quality of the soil it went into, or whether it was nurtured and watered.

You might have heard it said that the best time to plant a tree was twenty years ago. Well, the best time to believe and sow God's Word was when you heard it. The next best time is now. Right now. You might be looking for a harvest in your future. Do you have something planted? Do you believe God's Word now, or just when you want it to be true? Nothing is impossible to them that believe.

Sovereign Saviour

Who really is our Heavenly Father? The perception we have of Him has a big influence on us. It not only changes how we receive from Him, but far more importantly, how we show Him our love and steward what He invested (His Son). A wrong view can lead to costs you don't want to pay (Matthew 25:14-30). When we get a deeper revelation of who He is, it also transforms how we see ourselves.

Of everything in this book, the message of this chapter has the most potential to grow people's love of Him, love of others, make the Bible easier to understand, and increase our desire to live as God hopes.

The second half is where I want to focus, but I believe we need to journey through some stuff to get there. This could be compared to driving a long way to a destination, then finding out there were gears other than first. You may still get there, but some knowledge would have made the journey much better.

Is God making everything happen?

A big question to ask – it took rather extreme circumstances for me to sincerely face it.

One option is where God does nothing, and just sits back to watch us fight it out. However, there is so much evidence in Scripture that this is not the case and that He is actively involved in our lives (John 3:16, 1 Peter 5:7, Philippians 1:6).

Another option is where He does everything, and we just live by sight. Again, there is a lot of evidence in the Word that this is not the case either (1 Corinthians 3:9, Matthew 5:16, Matthew 11:29, John 15:5).

Somewhere in between those two boundaries is the path we walk *with* God (Micah 6:8).

> *Therefore, do not be unwise, but understand what the will of the Lord is.*
>
> *Ephesians 5:17*

God used this verse from Ephesians to change my life.

While reading it, He highlighted that just because something was happening did not mean it was Him, and we are expected to know the difference. James 1:16-17 states we are not to be deceived when circumstances are not from His hand.

> *Declaring the end from the beginning, and from ancient times things that are not yet done, saying, My counsel shall stand, and I will do all My pleasure...'*
>
> Isaiah 46:10

Without a doubt He knows the future – He is outside of time and can prophesy it (declare). All that He chooses to happen, happens! *His* council shall stand, but not every council, not all. The fact He must state *His* means there is a 'not His'.

What God doesn't make happen, doesn't have to stand!

Whatever is not His will, is in the hands of those with authority as to whether it continues. This is both submitting (making what He wants what you do) and resisting. If the enemy tries to make something happen through you, or around you, you have authority over all his power to stop it (Luke 10:19).

Whatever is God's Word He watches over to perform (Jeremiah 1:12). Whatever is not His Word can be silenced (John 10:5). God is true to His Word and does what He says He will, and I am so grateful for that. He backs up His Word; it is forever settled. Do you back His Word, submit to it, persevere in it, and stand on it?

Is there a plan?

Before we tackle that one, we need to ask, "Does God always get what He wants?" He does in heaven, but on earth as it is in heaven?

I find that most people agree God is not causing everything, but when something does not go the way they think it should, instead of trusting Him, some lean on their understanding and try to reason their experience. Often at that point their response shifts from quoting verses like...

- Ephesians 5:17 – understand what the will of the Lord is.
- James 1:16-17 – don't be deceived as to what is from His hand.
- Colossians 1:9 – I pray you would be filled with the knowledge of His will.
- John 15:15 – I know what He is doing, because He is my friend.
- Matthew 6:10 – Your will be done.
- 1 Corinthians 2:16 – we have the mind of Christ.
- Romans 12:2 – renew your mind, then you will prove what is His will.
- 2 Corinthians 5:7 – we live by what we believe, not what we see.
- Etc.

...to saying, "It must be part of His plan," and quote Isaiah 55:8, saying His ways are higher (which was spoken to the unrighteous, not the saved), ascribing to God whatever happens.

Consider these two Scriptures.

> *The Lord is not slack concerning His promise, as some count slackness, but is longsuffering toward us, not willing that any should perish but that all should come to repentance.*
>
> *2 Peter 3:9*

and...

> *"Enter by the narrow gate; for wide is the gate and broad is the way that leads to destruction, and there are many who go in by it..."*
>
> *Matthew 7:13*

Long-suffering toward us means that He is giving us the opportunity to change our mind and choose differently. He gives us the choice for destruction, despite what He wants. He can even warn us when things will bring death, but we can still make choices that lead to it. God may have a plan for us (Jerimiah 29:11, Ephesians 2:10), but He lets us choose whether to walk in it.

> *...who desires all men to be saved and to come to the knowledge of the truth.*
>
> *1 Timothy 2:4*

God has desires, but on earth He lets us choose, and therefore does not always get what He wants. All have sinned (Romans 3:23)!

What can we choose?

Every command to do (or not do) something in the Word, is only necessary where we have the choice to obey. The Bible contains many instructions, meaning we have a lot of choice. If we are told not to get drunk on wine, then we have a choice to make. We need to find out what His will is and submit to it, and what to resist and wrestle (James 4:7, Ephesians 6:12).

The Bible is fairly clear on two things concerning this:

- One: God is undoubtedly sovereign (mentioned three hundred-and-four times in the NIV), and
- Two: He gave us choice.

Not everything is God; not everything is us

Let me mention briefly that I am aware words can have different meanings for people. For example, 'sovereign' is not used at all in the King James Version, so what do you mean when you say it?

I define God's sovereignty as His being answerable to no-one, being omnipotent, omniscient, outside of time, able to do anything, anywhere, at any moment. And He is not a man that He should lie – He keeps His Word. He gave us choice even when we do not make life-giving ones. If you can or have sinned, you make something happen that is not the will of God. If we don't have a choice, then we can't really sin.

Imagine for a moment Cain asking God why He (God) killed Abel after slaying him himself. What if Abel in heaven asked God why He (God) took his earthly life so early. Maybe God was just lonely and needed more angels in heaven? God knew what was in Cain's heart and that he needed to master the sin crouching at his door. He warned him, but still let Cain choose. After the act of murder, God did not say, "Thank you for doing My will." He said, "What have you done?"

Abel's death was not God's choosing, but Cain's.

Does God stop people sinning?

How many times is it recorded in the Word that God knew someone was going to sin, and He stepped in and stopped it from happening? God establishes our ways (Proverbs 16:9). Many don't like the results of their choices, but God choosing to stop sin before it happens…? I can only think of one or two cases in the Word that might be seen that way, but it is more evident that He was protecting people (e.g., Sarah, Abraham's wife), rather than stopping someone from sinning.

God honours His choice to let us choose

Does God have a plan?

The Bible doesn't exactly answer this, so neither can I. He has plans for us (Jeremiah 29:11, Ephesians 2:10), but 'a' plan? God had a plan that Jesus would open blind eyes, is not saying there was 'a' plan that involved Him creating blind eyes in the first place. He knew the future, that in the time of Jesus there would be blind eyes, and planned for Jesus to open them, but that is not the same as creating them.

People having a plan for firefighters to put out fires, is not saying they are lighting them.

What I do know is, whatever God decides to make happen, happens. At the same time, people can sin making God's desire *not* happen. God has a will – things that are pleasing to Him; a plan for us – but He has chosen to work with our choices as to whether that happens.

Romans 8:28 declares that He *works* all things together, not *watches* a plan unfold. He can, when certain conditions are met, bring about good from all things. I have heard it said that God will work so much good out of a bad situation, you will think He caused it.

Don't be deceived as to who caused it

He is for _us_, not for His *plan*. When you really grasp this, it becomes a much higher priority to work with and remain in Him, to know and walk in the plans He has for us, to develop our character, grow our faith, take opportunities to _give Him opportunity_, and to boldly approach His throne and receive all Christ paid for.

There are many points I could raise here, but so we can focus on the next part, I will summarise them:

- All things are possible to them that believe, not just the things that were part of the chosen plan.
- Everything is permissible, but not everything is beneficial.
- I am responsible to submit to His will, not surrender to His plan.
- I partner with God and take my position as a fellow worker (1 Corinthians 3:9) when I seek first His kingdom and pray His will be done.
- I persevere, am steadfast, enduring, exercise patience, live by faith, and sow, etc., to see His will done, and not just sit back and hope for the best.

What defines His will?

I had previously assigned everything to God's *plan*, thinking that whatever happened was His *will*, but now I understand them as two different things.

Sight does not define Him, His Word does

Finding ourselves not being able to do something does not mean that we couldn't. *If* we remain, *if* we believe, *if* we have faith, etc.; choices we make alter the effectiveness of our prayers. When the disciples failed to cast out a spirit in Mark 9:28 (i.e. not able to do something), did not mean that was God's will. Jesus still got it done where the disciples had failed.

Are we taking responsibility to be in a position to do His will? Or are we just calling our failure His will?

Numerous people will go directly from, "God didn't make it happen" to "God allowed it to happen". This definition of allowed is exactly the same as choosing for it to happen. Everything in your life is allowed, but as with Abel's death, God might not be the one choosing it. God did not choose sin and death to come into the world, but allowed Adam (gave him the choice) to eat from the wrong tree – which he did, even with the warning that it would bring death.

We really should change our wording from 'allowed it' to 'chose for it', if that is what we mean.

God did not decide for Abel to die. He chose for Cain to have choice, and Cain allowed (chose for) Abel's death. That completely changes the way I have viewed many things. If your brother can take your life despite what God wants, what else is allowed?

We know that we are of God, and the whole world lies under the sway of the wicked one.
1 John 5:19

The whole world is lying under the sway of the wicked one, and that does not sound like God is controlling everything. Given opportunity, He sure can stop it – even through you *if* you have faith. God is not saying this to make us worry or be anxious, but that we might be aware of the enemy's schemes.

Like Job, if we are not aware that some things are not God's choice, we will just sit and wait for a storm to pass that Jesus would have us rebuke.

Second Half

What choices has God put in our hands?

What became so blatantly clear to me was...

If I could make His will not happen, then I could cause it to happen

When we reach this understanding, we become so much more aware of the importance of our decisions.

God wants to *partner* with us to make His will happen on earth as it is happening right now in heaven. We are to pray His will be done, not vainly (without effect), but knowing it makes a difference. His will does not always happen on earth just because He wants it to. Now, it truly matters that we know what His will is. I want to make His will happen in my life, which means running according to the rules, being diligent, pressing and reaching for the prize, bearing fruit, and giving Him opportunity.

We are co-labourers!

*For we are God's fellow workers; you are
God's field, you are God's building.*

1 Corinthians 3:9

He desires that His Word, His seeds, bear fruit in the field of your life. We can work with Him to be a good soil that His Word can grow in, or we can be stony ground that makes it easy for the enemy to snatch it away.

Instead of being in a perpetual state of convincing myself I was surrendered, I had to find out what to submit to. Scripture is full of God showing us what His will is, but I had thought that whatever happened was His will, and I ignored it.

It doesn't matter who you are, this applies to you!

Just because I failed to make His will happen at times in my life, didn't mean that it was not His will that it happened. This matters a great deal in healing and deliverance. I will talk about healing specifically, but people are calling their failure to minister His will, His will.

Just because you couldn't, doesn't mean He wouldn't

Does God want us strong?

I want to finish this chapter by stating very clearly that God wants us strong! Strength is our ability to prevail over resistance. Regardless of who we think is providing the resistance in our life (God or the devil), it is an opportunity to develop our character. The outcome should be the same.

Imagine being at the gym, only every time you attempted to lift a weight, your personal trainer replaced it with a smaller one. Instead of getting stronger, you get comforted with success in doing less. Every time you lift your head to do a crunch, they put a pillow under your head and encourage you to rest.

The allure of seeking comfort (reducing resistance) is robbing people from increasing their strength, and it can lead to an incredible amount of sin. The Bible is clear that we should take both joy in resistance and persevere in it (James 1:2, Romans 5:3, 2 Corinthians 12:10, 1 Peter 1:6, 1 Timothy 6:12, Philippians 3:14, etc.).

> *You therefore must endure hardship as a good soldier of Jesus Christ.*
>
> *2 Timothy 2:3*

You must 'choose to endure', not, be ready to receive hardship.

The culture today seems so set on being comfortable that they will pay nearly any price for it, be it time, money, health, even hurting others, etc. I don't have an issue with being comfortable, but it becomes an issue when the desire for it is put above faith, and faith gets compromised in its pursuit. For example, it could be something as simple as lying to defend your identity. Who do we serve – comfort or righteousness?

We must not be so focussed on being strong that we lose sight of His grace and mercy. However, they do not give us an excuse to stay weak.

Being weary means we have used our strength. He gives strength to the weary. He gives us the strength (grace) we need to overcome, conquer and prevail when we work with Him. God has already defeated the devil but wants us to be strong, victorious, and to crush him under our feet.

Take opportunities to test your faith; don't just look for a way to escape (be comfortable). Consider it pure joy when an opportunity presents itself to test your faith (James 1:2). Develop your character. Get strong.

Who do you represent?

We are Christ's ambassadors, and our God is strong. It matters to me that I am strong too. Not for my glory, but that I may represent my God well. On judgment day, God is not going to ask me if I made *my* name great, but His name. We are Christ's representatives. If you had to represent your country in something, you would probably take that seriously. You are representing God right now. How important is that to you? If I look at you, can I see who you represent? Can I see the Father?

Nowadays I pay more attention when the Bible talks about developing character, becoming stronger, sowing, and being faithful in the small. It's possible to lack nothing and be fruitful in our knowledge of Him (James 1:4, 2 Peter 1:8). I want that! Who chooses if we remain in Him, stay connected, draw near, approach the throne, spend time with Him, and be in His Word? God? God could have anything He wants, so how much of your heart does He have?

He jealously yearns for your heart, not forcefully takes it

Let's be real, nothing is impossible for God, and if you have faith, nothing will be impossible for you (Matthew 17:20). Mark 16:17-18 says that there are things that will follow those who believe. How should we believe? God is sovereignly allowing us the choice of what we sow. Are you sowing what you want to reap in the future, or just assigning what happens to 'God's plan'?

Choice, Not Free Will

Picture being in a bakery surrounded by a large range of beautifully decorated and great-smelling cakes. Some of them seem so good, you decide to buy one. Peering a bit closer, you notice there are no price tags anywhere, so you decide to engage with the person behind the counter. "Excuse me, how much are these?" They respond, "One is yours at no charge, but it will cost you." Puzzled, you reply, "What does that mean? If it's free, then it's free, right?" To which you hear, "No, you will pay the price of missing out on the cakes you don't choose." What do we miss out from assuming our choices are free?

Now picture being in a garden with many fruit trees. You hear a voice saying, "Eat this, it will make you more like God." What is the cost? You might miss out on the Tree of Life. How do we know what choices to make?

Free? Why do so many call it *free* will? Are they unaware their decisions cost? Just because everything is permissible does not mean it is free. Jesus paid a massive price for the choice of man. The more I consider that, the less desire I have to call it free will at all. Our decisions have a lot more cost than we may be aware of. The choices some people make today could have an eternal cost. Receive Christ's redemption, or not. The choice is yours, but it is far from free.

Like putting something on credit, it might be gratifying now, but it is going to cost you later. Imagine putting something very expensive on credit that you didn't actually want, and you couldn't return it. Wouldn't it be great if someone paid your debt?

God gave us choice

It is fairly evident in Scripture that you can do all the good you want, but no man comes to the Father except through Jesus. However, people receive this free (to them) gift of grace and become so confused about what matters anymore that they question if they should go on sinning. As Paul says, No! What matters now is living life with God.

Place 'Eternal life is that we might know Him' (John 17:3) with 'Depart from me I never knew you' (Matthew 7:23). Do you want to know God? He wants (is longsuffering) to walk with you!

> *To them God willed to make known what are the riches of the glory of this mystery among the Gentiles: which is Christ in you, the hope of glory.*
>
> *Colossians 1:27*

I am telling you as plainly as I know how, that you can make not only a choice that will gain you entry into heaven,

Christ in you, opening the door, laying the foundation, beginning to know Him, but also an ongoing choice to know Him more, to walk with Him, let Him be fully formed in your heart, and let your light shine brighter.

> *Do you not know that to whom you present yourselves slaves to obey, you are that one's slaves whom you obey, whether of sin leading to death, or of obedience leading to righteousness?*
>
> *Romans 6:16*

This verse was (is) given to people hearing the message of grace, having their spirits sealed, receiving eternal life, getting their participation award, starting their race, and receiving Christ in them – but there was still death to be had. Death is not only the separation of your spirit from your body. God said to Adam, "In the day you eat of it you will surely die." Adam didn't suddenly drop to the ground… so what happened?

Adam and Eve were deceived into making a poor choice. They made a decision that was in no doubt sin (all have sinned), but I want to emphasise that it had a price tag. It was permissible (he could make the choice), but the result was not beneficial.

They were deceived into receiving death by the lie that eating of the tree would make them 'like God'. Doesn't that sound like a reasonable thing, to be like God? Some of the sin I am redeemed from was in knowingly not doing things God's way – not from being deceived. Or was I?

We can only speculate what Adam and Eve were thinking as they were deceived, but the *how* was in not recognising who they already were. They were already like God; they were made in His image. The enemy's scheme was using the allure of being like God to deceive them into doing what he wanted, obtaining death.

Now, born again, we are made of God (2 Corinthians 5:17), and as He is, so are we (1 John 4:17). And we still hear a voice saying, "Do this to be like God"! Are you being tricked into doing things with the allure of being more like God, but actually releasing death?

A thistle bush can try and bear figs all it wants, but it won't become a fig tree. A fig tree bears figs as a fruit of what it is. When you are born again, it's like you were a thistle bush, and God has made you anew into a fig tree. Now, once our nature has been changed, we are commanded to bear fruits of our new nature, worthy of our change, worthy of our repentance. Not to gain it, but because of it.

The fig tree's yield (your yield), however, is dependent on the soil in which it is planted. Born again, you do not need to do a single thing to be like God. All things are of God, but you can live in a way that bears more fruit. Be a good soil; remain in Him.

I would like to point out that God still took care of Adam and Eve. He still covered them (sent His Son while we were still sinners), but they had to leave the garden. God kept them from accessing the Tree of Life because of their decision. If death does not mean your body stops working, then what is life?

Today, once saved and sin is taken out of the equation, our access to life is restored. Jesus is life. Is something keeping you from him? Behold, I stand at the door and knock. People will invite Him into their house (Christ in them), but instead of sitting at His feet like Mary (being good soil), they stay busy like Martha (choked by the cares of life).

What did God say no to?

A big impact on my life was when I realised that God said, "Don't eat of that tree, because it's not good for you, it brings death." He did not say, "If you eat of it, I'll kill you." This is such a big message to touch on, but I trust Holy Spirit to work it for good, and I will share only how it relates to this chapter's message.

Right and wrong exists, the tree was there, but it was not God's desire for man to feed on it. Don't eat that! I have stuff in my house and garden that I would say exactly the same about.

As born-again Christians, we should be renewing our minds to reckon ourselves dead to sin (no longer driven/filled/motivated with right and wrong) but instead, be setting our minds on life and peace (1 Peter 2:24, Romans 6:11, Romans 8:6).

> # Focussing on right and wrong brings death, it condemns me, and judges you

> *For with what judgment you judge, you will be judged; and with the measure you use, it will be measured back to you.*
>
> *Matthew 7:2*

The command God gave me was to love you, not make you meet my perception of right.

This is the key thing I want you to hear: If you fail to do the 'right' thing (miss the mark), it is sin – and the cost of it was already paid for by Jesus. Should we go on sinning then? No! Make it your goal to do the *life* thing (eat and get your fill from the tree of life), not the 'right' thing (the other tree). If you do not choose to do something that brings life (sow), don't blame God when you don't have it (reap).

> *For to be carnally minded is death, but to be spiritually minded is life and peace.*
>
> *Romans 8:6*

This verse clearly reveals the cost of where we keep our thoughts and imaginations. Where you keep your mind is your choice. The enemy is trying to influence (roaming, scheming and swaying) where you keep your mind (1 John 5:19) and would love to keep you religiously eating the fruit of right and wrong, trying to be like God. God already made you right, stop setting your mind on trying to be right! Instead, set your mind on what gives life. Jesus came to bring life (John 10:10).

> *For God did not send His Son into the world to condemn the world, but that the world through Him might be saved.*
>
> John 3:17

Jesus did not come into the world to point out the wrong it had done, but to help people have life.

We need to be shaken, woken, alerted to the fact that some things have a very real cost. If you focus on right and wrong, the cost of missing the mark, I repeat, that is simply another sin Christ died for. When your focus is life, you are deciding how much you walk with God. What does having less God in your life look like? Death?

What is the cost?

In the natural people have an idea what something is worth, whether it is a small cost like a cup of coffee, or a big cost like a new car. But in the spiritual, many seem to have no idea. We know what a loaf of bread costs, but how much would you pay to hear God's guidance on a job offer or choosing a spouse?

What is the price of peace, or ministering in healing or deliverance? If you could raise someone from the dead, would that be worth investing in? God has put a price on things, but people are deceived into thinking they don't have to pay it, that all the promises are yes and amen, and free. They think they can just beg God to give them what they want, when they want it. Then, if they don't get it, they will reason it wasn't God's will in the first place, and all His promises are only yes when He says so.

What makes something God's will? Is it only what happens, or is it what He says? Just because you fail to receive, doesn't mean He failed to provide. If God were to put hot fresh food on the table and say, "Help yourself," don't go to your bedroom and pray "If it be Thy will may it come to me." Just do what He says!

Luke 14:28 speaks about counting the cost of following Him. We want more of what Jesus had in His life, to follow in His footsteps and to do what He did, but are we willing to pay anywhere near the price He paid? How about a fast or giving up your sleep to spend time with the Father. Before we decide to sell all, can we even pay a price (make a choice) as little as planting His Word in our heart? If we want life (to see more of God's will on earth) we must count the cost (Luke 14:28), deny ourselves (Matthew 16:24), pay the price (Matthew 13:46), remain in Him (John 15:5), seek first His righteousness (Matthew 6:33), set our mind on life and peace giving things (Romans 8:5-6), sow His Word (Hebrews 4:12), and buy from Him (Revelation 3:18).

Galatians 6:7 is where we hear about God's principle (spiritual law) of sowing and reaping. People don't choose to get the right seed, roll up their sleeves, sow it, and then convince themselves that if they reap or not is God's choice. I have a garden. Imagine if I got angry at God for not having tomatoes or strawberries when I never planted any. God is not mocked. If you want to reap something, you should find out what to sow. People sow mindlessly, watching whatever is on TV or their phone, and want to reap the fruit of remaining in Him. Then, if they don't get it, they blame God for the outcome, saying it was His will.

Are you sowing?

We have the _choice_ of what we sow but are we planting what we want to reap from. People seem to be able to comprehend the idea of sowing and reaping bad things but seem to think that good only happens when God wants it to and that they aren't responsible for sowing. A large portion of the body of Christ as I know it are basing the will of God on what they are failing to reap, regardless of whether they are willing to sow.

Sowing

What is sowing?

We are God's field (1 Corinthians 3:9). I view sowing in two key ways. Doing things that invite God to be part of my life (loving God) and doing unto others (loving people). The rest of this chapter focusses on the former.

I _intentionally_ make choices to walk with and remain in Him, to _give Him opportunity_ to plant and grow fruit in the field of my life.

John 15:5 says that if we remain in Him, a _choice_ we make, we will bear much fruit. This is increasing in His character, growing into the fullness of Christ, living as a son of God, and all things being possible. What is the cost of having the fruit? It's not praying for it; it is remaining in Him.

When considering the fruit of the Spirit, you may notice they are character traits. They are things we increasingly become. They grow, they are not just things we do or don't have. Do we want to be more loving, kind, and to have more peace? Then we must remain in Him. God is merciful, and might give unplanted fruit occasionally, but it is not how He would prefer us to live. I know I want to have more joy in my life, so I choose to spend more time with Him and let that fruit grow.

How much time are you intentionally spending with Him? Five minutes of prayer a day will not have more effect than the twenty-three hours and fifty-five minutes of being unaware of His presence. The goal is to walk humbly with our God, not just meet up with him for sprints when it suits us (Micah 6:8).

When I reflect on the life of Jesus, I see there were times He stayed up all night with His Father, times set apart and devoted to Him, but in between He lived 'remaining.'

How do we remain in Him?

Here are some ways we can remain in Him. These are things we must be _intentional_ about. We don't always like the process of sowing, but we are not likely to complain about the harvest.

> **This is not about doing right, but doing what brings life**

Faith comes by hearing – Romans 10:17

We are not likely to know now the full extent to which the Father has been calling us on earth, but we know that He does (John 6:44). Who knows just how long He was speaking before we finally heard Him. The very start of our faith journey begins when we answer His call to repentance. Hearing His voice is how we receive Him. As we have received Him, so walk in Him (Colossians 2:6).

This may seem harsh, and I am immediately convicted as I write it, but I believe with all my heart that if we are not hearing Him then we need to act. Make opportunity. There is no right way to hear Him, but it is unlikely to happen if we are not listening. I heard Him in a song lyric, and it immensely changed my life. We can hear Him in our thoughts, our heart, in His Word, from other people, in songs or books, etc., but are we listening? I often hear Him when I am writing. If we are just trying to be 'Christian' (like God) and not listening for Him, then really, we are just undertaking religious activities, and likely obtaining death (less God).

Pray without ceasing – 1 Thessalonians 5:17

Prayer is such a misunderstood word, so when I say prayer, I mean talking _with_ God, not talking to Him. Following on from the first point, the goal is relationship, to know Him, not to get your needs met. When praying, do you ask Him anything besides what you would like Him to do? If so, do you believe you receive when you ask, and give Him the space to answer? When the disciples couldn't cast out a devil, Jesus's answer wasn't, "Sorry, I didn't know what you were saying," it was, "Your believing is wrong." Talking with God will fix that. Pray (sow)!

Jesus understood that the Father always heard Him (John 11:42). Are you aware that God always hears us? You can choose to talk with Him anywhere, anytime, not just in scheduled quiet times. We can learn to recognise and hear His voice, but once we know it, we can hear Him every moment of every day. We choose how often to talk with Him, and we don't need to be in our favourite chair to do so.

Read His word – Hebrews 4:12
His Word is alive and active, not just ink on a page. It is actively working in the lives of the people who plant it. Are you planting it and giving it the opportunity to be active in your life?

It would be a challenge to put my finger on a specific harvest from reading my Bible, but I know that the devil is so concerned about God's Word having the opportunity to take root that he tries to snatch it. We need to be active ourselves (intentional) in getting it planted. If you could see birds or bugs trying to get in your garden, you would put things in place to protect your crop. Are you that way with God's Word? His Words are seeds that properly planted and nurtured will bring a much-wanted harvest in your life.

Know what it says, but don't just be hearers of the Word. Remaining in Him is making His Word flesh in us. Don't just make His Word information stored in your brain – make it how you live. If you read your Bible, that's awesome, but if you close the book and forget what it says, it's like a man who looks in a mirror and forgets what he looks like as he walks away.

Spend time in worship – Psalm 22:3
Back when Adam and Eve first sinned, their eyes were opened to the flesh. God says that the mind set on the flesh is death. I find it interesting that God told Adam, "In the day you eat of the tree you will surely die," and after they ate, they saw their flesh, their nakedness.

Worship is an intentional act of setting your mind on something that is not flesh. God is spirit. The greatest commandment is to love God. I'm not talking about singing the songs you like, but the way you live (by faith). When you talk with Him, do you spend any time blessing His Holy name, or are you too focussed on sharing your needs? He knows your needs before you ask; they are not as big a deal as He is.

Here's a question more people need to ask: "Father, is there something you want to do through my life today?" Paul pleads with us to offer our body. Give Him something to do His will through (Romans 12:1)! In some translations, this is spiritual worship.

God dwells in the praises of His people! When you praise Him, you are inviting Him into your life. He jealously wants an invitation. He is standing at the door hoping you will open it. Let Him in.

Spend time with His people – Hebrews 10:25
In the natural, when you are with a group of people who are looking at something, you want to look too. This is the same with setting your mind on God. Get yourself among people who are looking to Him and you'll find yourself wanting to join them. God gave us people who are stronger in areas to build us up in the faith, and to grow and strengthen us until

Christ Jesus, the perfect man, is formed in us (Galatians 4:19). Put yourself in places where you are built up. Are you aware that going to a prayer meeting, a home group, a midweek service (sowing life-giving things) will bring a much better harvest than watching a screen?

Don't just hang with people who declare they have a ticket to heaven, but choose to be around those who seek to know God on earth, who are intentional about transformation, and who manifest Him in their lives. Not just hearers of the word, but doers. Bad company corrupts good character (1 Corinthians 15:33). This doesn't just apply to spending too much time with those who don't profess to believe yet, but also to those who call themselves Christian but look nothing like Christ.

Listen to the Word in truth – John 17:17, Ephesians 4:15

This is such an important one. Don't allow people – not me, not anyone – to deceive you into believing their reasoning in place of God's Word. I had to unlearn so much, and that is a lot harder to do than being discerning of what we should be learning in the first place. If it is different to God's Word, it is wrong. Sowing seeds that are not God's Word will change what you harvest. Imagine wanting to harvest corn, but the label on the seed packet was wrong and you planted radish instead. Now you must plant again, and you could be waiting twice as long for a harvest.

Pray in tongues – Jude 1:20

Speaking in tongues is such an amazing gift. It has made a huge difference in my life, and I can't easily explain it. But I am so built up by it. As an example, teaching coming to me, through me, and there is no natural way that I could know some stuff. My earthly grey matter is just not that clever. It is something I sow because I know that Holy Spirit brings a greater harvest in my life.

Let others prophesy over you – 1 Thessalonians 5:20
Sometimes we just need to have the Word spoken over us by others. Do not despise prophecy. We are a body with many members, and each of us have different strengths. Some people have more experience in prophecy, others in healing (elders), deliverance (casting out devils), and hearing a word of knowledge. We are to build each other up, stir one another to faith and good works – iron sharpening iron.

There are so many ways that we can remain in Him. God is not the one making that choice. We are!

Submit, Not Surrender

This is quite a controversial subject to challenge, but I feel strongly about it. I don't want to meaninglessly fight about words, but to challenge what is believed when using them. I was all about that surrendered life for a long time, until I realised His will was something to fight for. For me, this chapter is about action versus inaction. My hope is that people would read this and feel a conviction to be more submitted, not to condemn people for their understanding of surrender.

Should I be surrendered?

Being surrendered seemed to me a good Christian way to live. With so many songs, books and teachings, I thought I was honouring God by being surrendered… but was I? It's almost as though surrender is every second word for some Christians. Is that really what God wants from us? Would Jesus walk in the room and say, "You would be a better follower of mine if you were more surrendered"?

How would you define surrender? I surveyed a reasonably sized group to gain a better understanding of what is generally believed about surrender, and apart from a couple of responses, people liked the 'let go and let God' definition.

The way I see this reasoning is by picturing Jesus saying, "Come, follow me," but I can't because I am too consumed in a tug of war for my future, so I surrender. I put down the rope, let go, and let God take it for me. I say, "God, I trust you with my future, whatever that is, and I won't resist it." This thinking doesn't give any consideration to following Him, and ultimately, it is only about my will. I've just changed who I deem responsible for it.

This does not sound right.

What does the Bible say?

I would have thought that for the number of times surrender is mentioned in Christian circles, it would be all through the Bible. Much to my surprise, I found it is not. It is found zero times in the New Testament of the King James Version, and – even more unexpectedly – zero times in the New Testament of the New International Version. Look it up! This should raise a flag for us.

In other translations, we find surrendering one's body to be burnt as being worthless if we don't have love (1 Corinthians 13:3), and another verse says they did not surrender (to false brethren) (Galatians 2:5).

This is where people may try to defend the concept of surrender with their own definition, but is it Scripture? We all could probably come up with a definition that satisfies, but it is more important to me to follow the Bible than my reasoning.

In the Old Testament, surrender is used to mean I will not struggle as you take my life or enslave me. It is a way to declare that you give up fighting or resisting, that you have lost hope of winning the battle.

'Biblical' surrender is to an enemy, God is not your enemy!

Who are you surrendering to?

If you are fighting not with God but the devil, surrender is not an option.

We are to:

- wrestle against the kingdom of darkness (Ephesians 6:12)
- prevail (Matthew 16:18)
- overcome (1 John 5:4-5)
- be more than conquerors (Romans 8:37)
- be strong (Joshua 1:9)
- be led into victory (2 Corinthians 2:14)
- stand, when we have done all else – not surrender (Ephesians 6:13).

Reflecting on the story of Jacob wrestling with God in Genesis 32:22-29, did Jacob surrender? No. Even with his hip out of joint, he said, "I am not letting go until you bless me." We don't need to wrestle with God any more to get blessed, we have already been blessed (Ephesians 1:3), but will we boldly approach His throne and claim our inheritance?

What does 'deny yourself' mean?

Matthew 16:24 says if we want to follow Him, we must first deny ourselves. People may call this surrender, but it is submission, and it only means something if you are going to follow Him. It states that you are willing to pay a cost to go His way. If you are not going to follow Him, then you might as well drink wine and be merry, serve mammon and your belly. At the end of the day, what does it matter?

Should we use this word if the Bible doesn't?

In my own life I do not want people surrendered to me. Surrender means I have conquered their will, so now they do what I say regardless of whether they want to. As a parent this could be asking your child to sit down. They might obey, but in their heart they are still standing. Imagine asking a friend to help you move house, then finding out they didn't want to but their spouse made them do it. I would much rather people *want* to help me out than discover they surrendered and did something they were made to do. It seems almost shocking to say – like using a dirty word – but truthfully, I would rather have my wife submit to me than to surrender.

We are the bride of Christ. Does He really want a surrendered bride? Or a submitted one?

If I were to use the word surrender (which I think is the wrong word), this is how I would picture it. Imagine swinging on vines, like Tarzan through the jungle. Jesus hands you another vine and says, "Come follow me," but the only way to take the vine He is giving you is to surrender the one you are on. There is no option where you just let go of your vine and *not* take His. If you do that you will fall to the forest floor.

Some people try to take hold of both His vine and theirs. This is such a bad decision, pulling you in two different directions, creating tension and stealing your peace. Eventually, you will become weary and still have to choose… either come to Jesus or stick with your vine (your will). If you choose to stick with your vine, the most you can do is swing around and go nowhere.

Why does it matter?

I would say the most dangerous thing about surrender is no longer fighting (believing) for an outcome in your future. This means you can't show evidence of it (Hebrews 11:1), which makes it hard to have faith for it. Surrendering your future and saying that you trust God with it means that you're not asking for things with faith, believing that you receive them when you ask. You do not have because you do not ask (James 4:2). You can, and should, keep asking for things in your future, but they should not be more important than doing His will.

If you think you can surrender at the same time as asking, seeking, knocking, fighting the fight, running the race, pressing, reaching, conquering, overcoming, persevering and standing, I don't think we agree on the same definition of surrender. I will not surrender trying to accomplish my Father's will, even though it might cost me everything.

Replacement

What does He want?

If our Father is not asking us to surrender, what is He asking? To submit! This is actually given to us as an instruction to live by in James 4:7. I make my will to do the Father's.

Submission, like repentance, is a change of direction. I won't go my way, but I choose to go Yours. When we consider the life of Jesus in the Garden of Gethsemane (Luke 22:42), He did not say, "You do what You want, and I'll try and have peace about it." It was a choice to do His Father's will, knowing full well what that meant. That is why He was sweating drops of blood.

What you want, that I do!

For Jesus, doing His Father's will was more important to Him than saving His life. Love not your life unto death (Revelation 12:11)! To do this, you need to know what it is you are submitting to. You can surrender without any effort to do the Father's will, but you cannot submit to God without knowing His will and making a choice to go the direction that accomplishes it.

Surrender says, "I am not sure what you are going to do, but I know You are good, so however I experience life going forward is what you desire for me." Be careful on that one. James 1:13 tells us that some things have nothing to do with God. James 1:16-17 says don't be deceived, not all things are from God's hand.

Submission, alternatively, says, "I know what You want" (Ephesians 5:17), and if something doesn't look like that in my life – like how Jesus lived or like heaven on earth – I am going to exercise faith to see it change, even if it costs me time, energy, money, or pride, etc. Jesus said, "I only do what I see the Father doing" (John 5:19), "I am about my Father's business" (Luke 2:49), and "Not My will, but yours be done" (Luke 22:42).

Surrender is about your will; submission is about His

The biblical definitions, which are quite important if we want biblical results, is that surrender is an action you take in relation to an enemy, while submission is your action to serve a master.

I personally believe that the reason so many use the term surrender is that they are deceived, like I was, into believing that a master plan was going to happen regardless of what they did, and the best way to live was surrendered to it.

I can't tell you where this doctrine came from, but regardless of my understanding, the Bible is telling us to live like what we do will be worked together, and to live by faith, not by sight.

What is yielding?

There is one more thing to discuss on this subject, which is to yield. Yielding, like surrender, is one of those words that isn't used much in the Bible, but lots in Christianity. I can only suggest what it means to me and pray the Holy Spirit leads us into truth, but when I think of yielding, I think of presenting.

To me, it is a choice to give to God, i.e. to present our bodies. It is a decision to put something in His hands knowing full well that he is sovereign, wiser, and stronger than we are. It is not a choice to say, "What will be, will be," but is to ask God to show us His will, the way forward, to guide our footsteps, direct our paths, and be our teacher. The Bible says to keep asking!

At the end of the day, whose will do you want to happen? I submit to God and seek Him for the path He wants me to walk in accomplishing His will. Although surrender might sound like a good thing to say, submit is what the Bible says, and I encourage you to live by that.

Resist, Rest, Repeat

Until we admit that some things are not the will of God, not His choice, and can be changed, then there really is nothing to resist. If we think everything is part of God's master plan, then surrender might be a good option. If not, when we know something is not God, that is when we truly start questioning if we can do anything about it.

Imagine signing up to fight in a war. The General issues you all the defensive gear you need and a weapon to fight with. But not knowing how to put it on or use your weapon, you just head to the front lines without them. You think, "The General knows what he is doing. If this battle gets tough, I'll just call on him to help me." Hold on a moment… wasn't it him who gave you the armour in the first place?

If He told you to wear it, find out how to put it on!

We are told in James 4:7 to resist the devil! If you look at other uses of the Greek word for resist, it is clearly not just to defend, it is also to oppose (withstand, come against). Ephesians 6:11 says to put on the armour of God so we can.

Can we put on the armour, if we don't know what it is?

Trying to answer this question was where this book started. While writing my previous book someone questioned the nature of salvation, and I remember thinking at the time, "If you don't know you're saved, how can you put the helmet on?" Can you know you're saved?

Belt of Truth

Before you can put on any of the armour, you must prepare yourself (gird up) by knowing what the truth is. God's Word is truth (John 17:17). Until this choice is made, you will be tossed to and fro by whatever reasoning sounds (or sight looks) good at the time, and it may actually prevent you from receiving what God has provided (James 1:8).

When you make the choice to believe God's Word as truth, then you must choose to follow what it says (live by faith). In my own life, it made me so free to just ask of any theology, "Is it God's Word?" If not... thanks, but no thanks. His Word tells us what to believe (run according to the rules). Don't allow somebody's reasoning of their experience to take the place of God's Word and become a stronghold in your life. Without the Word, we wouldn't even know what the armour was. If it was good enough for Jesus, it's good enough for me. It is written!

Breastplate of righteousness

Jesus made you right (2 Corinthians 5:17-21). Stop trying to *be* right, by *doing* right. Instead, set your mind on life and peace (Romans 8:6). Like Jesus, make it your aim to bring life (John 10:10). Let making peace guide your choices (Colossians 3:15).

Gospel of Peace

Peace is such good news, but what is it? It is not the gospel of a preferred feeling. I say a few times in this book that it really is not important for you to believe what I do, but that you know what you believe, and you live it. God can direct your steps and lead you into all truth (Philippians 3:15), but you have to take a step that He can direct. Is it your desire to walk towards being in the truth that makes you free? Are you taking any steps, like reading the Word?

The gospel of peace is reconciliation, making people one with God. I have shared what peace means to me ahead, and it is news I want to share.

Shield of Faith

Above all, live what you believe. The enemy is scheming and swaying, shooting fiery darts of deception, and trying his best to stop you living in the truth.

What do you believe? We live by faith, which means we have already decided what we believe (belt of truth). We should know what the truth is, and not reduce it to something we agree with, close the Book, and forget what it says. We must make his Word flesh by how we live.

If you don't know the truth, the devil may trick you into eating a fruit that brings death

Helmet of Salvation

This is listed as our last piece of defensive armour. I believe this order is significant. We are to know that we have a ticket to heaven, but we shouldn't make that the most important thing in our lives. We need to put on the helmet of salvation, but set our minds on life and peace (Romans 8:6), being transformed, and loving God and others, not on being sorted when your time on earth is up.

- Christ died for all (1 John 2:2)
- Whomever can receive it (John 3:16)
- God wants everyone saved (2 Peter 3:9)
- Receive His gift free by faith (Ephesians 2:8)
- No works required to receive it (Ephesians 2:9)
- Once you have it, bear fruit of it (Matthew 3:8)
- Find out and do what God has planned for you (Ephesians 2:10)
- Let the redeemed of the Lord say so! (Psalms 107:2)

If you are saved, make yourself say so!

Sword of the Spirit (the Word of God)

The last bit of equipment we are given is offensive (not defensive)! Stick (pierce) the Word of God where it needs to be heard.

When the devil aims a fiery dart at you, quench it by living in truth (shield of faith), but then respond (attack back) with "It is written…"! To do this you must know what that is. The devil is overcome by the Blood of the Lamb and the word of our testimony. It's partnership; we must do our part. Sometimes we need to hear it ourselves (mind renewal), and sometimes we need to speak it for others (go about).

How should we start resisting?

The most effective way to resist the devil is to be in submission to God. This can be described as making it priority to know Him, His will, His Word, renewing our mind, seeking first His kingdom, understanding His righteousness, putting on the armour provided, and taking up our cross.

When we choose to make submission a priority, God's will (choice) becomes clearer, and whatever is not His will becomes much more obvious. This is when, in submission, we start to determine what we should resist. I had previously, in ignorance, thought everything was somehow God, so I didn't resist much at all. I let the devil get away with pretty much anything he wanted, and I paid some hefty costs because of that. Find a work of the enemy and join the war to destroy it. Your words have power. Add to the force of God's Word by knowing His will (Ephesians 5:17) and by praying it be done on earth as in heaven.

There are many verses referring to the varying effectiveness of our prayer. *If* you have faith, *if* you believe, according to the power working within you, the effective fervent prayer of the righteous avails much. The reason I mention these Scriptures is that our prayer is so much more effective when we are fully persuaded by what we believe (belt of truth). When we know we are not fighting God, we fight very differently, even fervently. We will persevere, endure hardship like a good soldier, and will very likely have more victories (Hebrews 6:12). That's worth our consideration.

Wearing the armour, establishing a hedge of protection, and renewing our mind, makes it so much harder for the devil to get into our life. We can also take to kicking him out of the lives of others and destroying his works. This can be natural, e.g., feeding the hungry and going about doing good, OR supernatural, e.g., casting out devils, healing the sick, and removing the oppression of the devil (Acts 10:38). Act according to your faith. "What I have, give I thee."

Where is he? On the doorknob?

The devil is not omnipresent (everywhere all at once) but the kingdom of darkness sure tries to appear that way. When I say the enemy or the devil, I am referring to the kingdom of darkness, a group, not a singular entity. The devil is roaming about and frequents the places he has acquired a foothold. This is why we are warned not to give him one. Does he have a place in your life to come and go as he pleases, like having his own key to your house?

Is God choosing for you to face trials or temptations?

I believe the story (historical record) of Job causes much turmoil for people. It seems many tend to picture the story of Job as the devil asking for permission to make Job's life hard, and God choosing for it to occur. Firstly, the devil did not need God's permission to put Job through the trial; he already had license when God allowed him choice. The devil is going about seeking whom he may devour and is looking for a foothold in our lives to take advantage. Who is doing the resisting in your life? In Job's life, God was. God was stopping the devil at every turn; He provided Job a hedge of protection. If the devil wanted to get to Job, then he had to talk to God.

To get my point across, Cain did not need to ask for permission to kill Abel. He already had license. We see Cain resisted when God warned him to master the sin at his door. For thought... was Job deserving of any more resistance than Abel? We might not know how much God is resisting in our lives, but if the devil asks God not to, can we resist?

> *And the Lord said, "Simon, Simon! Indeed, Satan has asked for you, that he may sift you as wheat. But I have prayed for you, that your faith should not fail; and when you have returned to Me, strengthen your brethren."*
>
> *Luke 22:31-32*

Please note Jesus didn't just say no, he prayed for Peter to have strength. God wants you strong.

God provided Job with a hedge of protection, and as far as I understand, there was no covenant (agreement), no requirement for God to keep up his end of the deal. God was protecting Job because He wanted to. I don't know why He agreed to stop resisting on Job's behalf (maybe because He knew Job would make a spectacle of him), but regardless, the tide has now turned. The responsibility to resist has been given to us.

We are in a covenant! God tells us to resist. He says we should do it, and then gives us the ability to do it with authority over all the works of the enemy, trials, and temptations (Luke 10:19). That means we can renew our mind and develop our character to where we can resist the devil as much as God was doing for Job, i.e. all; every work. That doesn't mean we can right now, but that is what is achievable, and what we could be pressing and reaching for.

Two main things I personally get from the story of Job is...

- to not be confused about what is of God. Submit, as discussed earlier (Ephesians 5:17, James 1:16-17), and
- to see what an unresisted devil will do. Resist!

Resisting the enemy can be challenging to explain as it is so varied, so we will start with something basic. Say no to temptation. Say no to gossiping, having another drink, taking things that aren't yours, telling lies, eating unwisely. These are obvious temptations to some people, and giving into these may result in trials, like people getting hurt, drunken decisions, jail, broken trust and health issues.

You can say no to creating trials in the lives of others just by saying no to temptations in your own life. Your temptations can cause other people great trials. How much is giving into a temptation going to cost? Cain's temptation cost Abel his life. It could be broken families, loss of possessions or loved ones, unemployment, and on and on that goes. The devil longs to get you to put your desires above the wellbeing of others (pride).

The devil is prowling around looking for people who won't resist him or who will give up resisting him and surrender. We are not condemned when he deceives us – we do not hold on to the past – but being ignorant of his devices can cause a lot of pain. Don't give the devil a foothold, an inch of your life, a second of your thoughts. He will use it to do as much damage as he can. Resist him.

> *Do not be deceived, my beloved brethren. Every good gift and every perfect gift is from above, and comes down from the Father of lights, with whom there is no variation or shadow of turning.*
>
> *James 1:16-17*

Can I be deceived?

The Bible says very clearly we can be deceived. James wouldn't tell us not to be if we couldn't. One way is thinking a temptation is of God's choosing, and another is when we are misled as to where things come from. Not only does the devil tempt you to do things God doesn't want, he tries to get you to receive things (i.e. trials) convincing you they're from God. Good and perfect things come from the Father's hand; don't be deceived where bad stuff is coming from. No variation. There is a real issue today with people receiving things without any resistance at all because they are deceived that they're from God. He is a good Father! He will not give you a stone.

One scheme the devil often uses is to convince us that certain things that happen are just natural. What is *just* natural? We may debate this, but I strongly suggest you ask God before accepting something Jesus would heal or cast out. If it is a curse that His Blood has redeemed you from, resist it.

We need to, at the very least, question the source of things. If you are in doubt about where something is coming from, resist first and ask questions later. It is much better to have God tell you that you were resisting Him by accident than to receive something you weren't supposed to bear.

How do we resist?

As it is written...
Resisting the devil starts with submitting to God, but it is not all there is. Jesus, the most submitted person there was (is) still had to resist. We need to know what is written. What will do absolutely no good is to go by what is experienced, how it seems, or what he or she says. The devil knows the Scriptures, and boldly twists them. Just look at the way he tempted Jesus. He knows what has the weight of heaven

behind it, what has authority and power, and what he must bow his knee to.

The Word of God is a sword (Ephesians 6:17)! A sword is an offensive weapon. We need to know what to believe (shield of faith, belt of truth) when the devil attacks with some perversion of the truth, some deception, but then we attack back with what is written.

Pray
"But deliver us from the evil one" (Matthew 6:13). I don't claim to apprehend all the inner workings of the spiritual realm, but I am clued up enough to pray, "Thy will be done," and that more so when I know it isn't.

I do not always see the fruit of my tongue, but I have seen enough (tasted) to know my words have power (Proverbs 18:21). God can and does resist the devil on people's behalf; if He didn't, the world would be in a lot more trouble than it is. In the story of Job, we read that the devil was not allowed to take Job's life. There was a point at which he was resisted. However, if God resisted totally, one hundred per cent of the time, we would have no need of armour and never get to exercise our God-given authority. We need to do our part! God is not doing it all for you; He wants you to be strong. What is the degree that God is resisting in your life? I don't know where the line is in my life, but I know that God is for me and wants me to grow in my strength. I will do what I can and hope in His mercy for the rest.

Jesus gave us His Blood
They overcame him by the Blood of the Lamb and the word of their testimony (Revelation 12:11). Jesus has overcome the devil, but have or can you? The way I see it, His Blood is

His mercy. The Bible says we can overcome him once we are born again – but while I am renewing my mind to live in that truth, I am thankful for His mercy. God is for us, and strong where we are weak. The devil was defeated at the Cross, but God is still wanting to crush him under our feet. Let's do our part, speak our testimony (agreement with His Word), and trust in His mercy (His Blood) for where we are weak.

Wear God's armour

Ephesians 6:11 says to put on the *whole* armour of God that we may be able to resist the devil. The devil is looking for a weak point to attack us. We're not to put on part of the armour, but all of it.

Do good

Do not be overcome by evil but overcome evil with good (Romans 12:21). I just noticed as I write that Jesus went about doing good; in the context of this verse He went about overcoming evil. The significance of this verse to me is that resisting the devil is sometimes as simple as doing good. If the devil is trying to make someone worry about where their next meal is coming from, and you show up with it, his attempt to promote any fear or worry is overcome.

> *...For this purpose, the Son of God was manifested, that He might destroy the works of the devil.*
>
> 1 John 3:8

Resisting the devil is not just limited to our own lives. Acts 10:38 says that Jesus went about doing it. He healed all who were oppressed of the devil. Notice that verse does not say that some were excluded because their sickness was God's will or that they were being taught a lesson. Regardless of where you think sickness comes from, as followers of Christ we are to resist the devil for others. Jesus was not made manifest to defend Himself from the works of the enemy, but to destroy them. He came to bring a sword, not a shield (Matthew 10:34). Let's go on the offence and crush the devil whenever he tries to put his head up.

Rest

> *Come to Me, all you who labour and are heavy laden, and I will give you rest. Take My yoke upon you and learn from Me, for I am gentle and lowly in heart, and you will find rest for your souls.*
>
> Matthew 11:28-29

Should I rest?

The Bible clearly says that we must be diligent to enter His rest (Hebrews 4:11). What does that mean? Have I? Is this just a one-off thing, or ongoing? In the trial I have fallen into as I write, several people have encouraged me to rest. What do they mean? This caused a bit of frustration for me at the time, because I wanted to do the right thing but I didn't know what that was. If Jesus told me to rest, what would He be wanting?

Wrong understanding on rest is, in my opinion, one of the biggest contributors to unnecessary hardship. Instead of exhorting people to fight the good fight, resist the devil until he flees, persevere, and inherit promises, they are encouraged to read a good book and wait in surrender for the storm to pass.

In today's culture our body is priority number one, whereas the Bible says to offer our bodies as a living sacrifice. Paul says, "I discipline my body," and in Matthew we read, "Come to Me when you are weary." That makes this topic a challenging write.

I want to summarise my thoughts up front so people know where I stand.

I believe there is rest:

- for your body (John 4:6)
- for your soul (Matthew 11:29)
- in completing a task (Hebrews 4:10)

Rest for your body is like keeping your car oil topped up. Quite necessary at times but you only do it as required, and excess oil does not achieve much, and it occasionally makes a mess. Without vision (a reason to use oil) people perish (Proverbs 29:18). If you choose not to keep your oil level maintained, you can cause a lot of unnecessary damage. Some cars burn through more oil than others, but generally speaking, you can go a long way without having to intervene (time taken to get weary). There is not really any point in keeping your oil level right if you are not going anywhere. We keep the oil maintained so we can get to our destination – but we live by destinations, not by oil level.

Rest for your soul can be compared with knowing the way to your destination. You can save a lot of time, energy, frustration, and wear and tear on your car with just a little bit of knowledge. You get to decide how well you know the route, whether it is blindly following the opinions of others (like GPS) or actual directions in God's Word. There is no point in following those who keep arriving at the wrong place, i.e. they know the promises of God (destinations), but they don't arrive at them (never coming to a knowledge of the truth). You shall know them by their fruits. Learning the route may increase your motivation to use your car and go places, but will you go? Or just be a hearer?

Rest in the completion of a task is like arriving at your destination. Whether you take the scenic route or have to push your car the last few metres, does not matter. You may have had to change a tyre or get some petrol (persevere), but you made it. Many view the destination only as heaven, but it is heaven on earth. People usually know the promises (destinations) and can even know the route, but instead of taking the journey (belief, faith, and perseverance), they go on a picnic and call it rest.

Be diligent to get your car where it needs to go. Don't miss out on the rest that is available when you make your body follow the route in your soul (faith) and receive God's promises (heaven on earth). Know the way, but don't just leave your car polished in the garage. God is not impressed with how shiny your car looks. He looks at the heart and helps people who are pressing and reaching (persevering) towards the right destination (He directs us, not pushes us against our will). Like the promised land, the destination exists, but, due to unbelief, people don't always get there.

Don't just be hearers only, but be doers of the Word

Challenging the idea of rest for your body seems to get people fired up, but it is not as important as other types of rest. This may be why you won't notice much emphasis on it in Scripture... until you are weary. Biblically, rest for your soul is found in learning from Him (renewing your mind). Rest for your body is acquired as needed, whereas rest for your soul is ongoing and increases. People can at times need rest in their body or their soul because of believing the wrong things. This is why we need to learn from Him and find out what to believe.

When you hear rest, do you hear "Be refreshed" (recover), "Renew your mind" (learn from Him), or "Do what it takes to believe"?

When I hear rest, I hear believe!

What is rest?

It amazes me how often different Greek words are translated to one English word. The word 'rest' in Matthew 11:28, is not the same word for 'rest' in the very next verse. Then, the word for being diligent to enter His rest is different again.

I propose that rest for your body is what you do to recover from something, e.g. Jesus sitting at the well, or asleep on the boat in the storm. If you don't have anything to physically recover from (your oil gauge is still full), then I am not sure what you are trying to achieve by resting.

If a friend of mine was competing in a race, I might be handing out cups of water or doing whatever I could to help them compete for a prize, not encouraging them to quit in case they break a sweat. When the race was over, I may encourage them to allow their body to recover before taking on another race. Their believing may be wrong, e.g. their identity is wrapped up in running races, causing them to make poor choices with their body, e.g. pushing themselves too hard or not attending important life events. That is changed by renewing the mind (learning from Him), not taking up cycling.

Regarding rest, I feel God highlighted to 'run as one who competes for a prize'. This brings to mind the tortoise and hare story. Resting cost the hare the race. A race has a start and a finish. We get to choose what races we run at times (e.g. going on a specific mission or resisting something). In between we may get weary and have to go to Jesus, but we cannot have a rest when we are supposed to be running.

Imagine putting on a barbeque. Your belief in its purpose will determine how much of your body you are willing to put on the line. If you consider it only a nice gesture, you will be less likely to keep going when you get tired. But if you genuinely believe that people will die of starvation if you don't feed them, you may press on until you collapse from exhaustion. The desire to push your body is relative to your belief. There may be times when your body needs rest from labour, but if you truly believe God has called you to do it, you will find a way to renew your strength and jump back in.

Doing this every day of your life can be wearying on your soul, especially if you have doubts (tension) about your commitment to it. But if you genuinely believed that God wanted you to keep going while you were suffering, take it up with Him (James 5:13). At the end of the day, do you know what or who you are submitting to? If so, offer your bodies as living sacrifices, discipline your body, and endure hardship as a good soldier. Make sure you are believing correctly though, or the enemy may work you into the ground.

When I consider the life of Jesus, I see someone who lived unmoved by the way His body felt. It was not a point for discussion. He seemingly placed no value on the condition of His body. Should we? It was more important to Him to make His body serve what He believed, than to serve how His body felt. Jesus was moved by compassion, but this comes from what you believe, not a chemical reaction. What do you believe? Jesus believed in bringing life and destroying the works of the enemy, and made His body serve that purpose.

In one translation, Jesus says, "Come to Me all who are weary, and I will give you rest." Two things stand out to me in this verse. One is, "Come to Me," not "Go on holiday." It seems that there is more emphasis on going to anything the world has to offer, over spending time with the One who can give you rest. The other thing is that if we want rest, we are to come 'weary'. Are you weary, or is it something else?

And He said to me, "My grace is sufficient for you, for My strength is made perfect in weakness." Therefore, most gladly I will rather boast in my infirmities, that the power of Christ may rest upon me.

2 Corinthians 12:9

God says that His strength is made perfect in weakness. If people are not willing to be in a place where they are weak (or weary) but rather keep having rests, then they are likely limiting opportunities for God to be strong in them. Maybe if you allow yourself to be weak, then He can be strong, and likely do a lot more than you could ever do rested.

We are a body (many members), and together we offer our bodies as living sacrifices to see His will done. But how much of your body you personally offer will depend on what you believe. Jesus didn't offer only a portion of His body for you.

Rest for our souls comes as we learn from Him and renew our minds. He knows and wants to share with us the better way (route) and to disciple us. As we increase in rest for our souls (seek first, Matthew 6:33), worries about our body will be taken care of. The mind set on the spirit is life and peace; the mind set on the flesh (the body) is death.

My last point regarding rest, is the one I care the most about. Applying effort to believe.

God's Word is true, regardless of whether we believe it. The more we believe it, the more willing we are to put our bodies (our lives) on the line for it. Jesus believed all the way to the Cross. People say they believe, but faith without works is dead. Make your body do according to what you believe in your soul (faith).

My biggest issue with rest is letting my *body* tell me how to live, rather than by what I believe. I understand there are situations where people are weary, as per Matthew 11:28, and need to sit down, but I would encourage you to be diligent to enter the rest of believing before telling you to go to the beach.

How much do you believe God's word?

Using healing as an example (a destination), some don't believe in it at all, some believe enough to pray in a group, some will lay hands, some will come to your house, some will have meetings, some will temporarily move in with you, some may set up healing homes, and some will lay hands until their arms get sore.

The main variable here is belief. Are we being diligent to believe? How much will we put on the line? Will we pray, fast, read our Word, give our money, or attend prayer/worship/healing/deliverance meetings? Do we taste and see, test and prove, have faith that is an action? All things are possible to him who believes. How much do we believe God's Word?

In conclusion, did God rest?

Yes, He did! When was that? When He completed the task, the job was done. The Bible does not say He rested when He got tired, or when six days had passed. It doesn't say God started work again on the eighth day or the new week. He rested when He finished His task of creation.

Jesus said, "It is finished," then sat down

Aren't you glad that Jesus finished the race He came to earth to run? In Hebrews 4:11, we are commanded to be diligent to enter His rest, not be focussed on waiting for heaven. The whole chapter is basically on the topic of rest. The Israelites did not enter His rest due to unbelief. They were not prepared to believe His report and fight to possess the promise God had given to them. Has God given you a promise, but you're not willing to lift a finger for it, fight the fight, be diligent and believe God? We haven't *just* been promised a ticket to heaven.

We must beware that we aren't focussing on rest for our flesh at the cost of being diligent to enter the rest of believing. The tenth and eleventh verses of Hebrews 4 summarises most of what I am trying to say about rest. Get the work done as God did. What's the work? Believe (John 6:28-29)!

Faith, not Fate

Faith, not the religion you might be a member of, but the action of one's belief, is God's invitation to <u>partner</u> with Him and shape the future. Fate just goes along for the ride. God could make the future go any way He wants it to, be in control, but instead He has chosen to work with our faith.

> *For we are God's fellow workers; you are*
> *God's field, you are God's building.*
> *1 Corinthians 3:9*

'The just shall live by faith' (Romans 1:17, Galatians 3:11, Hebrews 10:38). It's not, 'Living by faith they shall become just'. Nor is it, 'However the just live, will be called faith'. It's that the people who have been made just, <u>choose</u> to live by faith.

You can choose not to live by faith, but what is the cost if you do?

> *...above all, taking the shield of faith with which you will be able to quench all the fiery darts of the wicked one.*
>
> *Ephesians 6:16*

Living by faith is not just encouraged, it protects and shields us.

What does it mean to live by faith?

If you can't define faith, then you can't live by it. You don't have to agree with my definition, but you must have one.

According to Hebrews 11:1, faith is the evidence (action) of things unseen (belief). James 2:17 says that faith (belief) without works (action) is dead. The definition I now hold is that faith is belief in action.

Faith is a way to live, not a thing to use

I used to view faith as my likelihood to get what I wanted, like knowing I had enough money to buy something without even knowing how much it cost. Faith does get you things, but it is a *fruit* of the way you live, not a quantity you muster up. *If* you remain in me, you will bear much *fruit*.

The gift of faith, is not like a gift card that gets you what you want for free. It's a boldness to act, believing God's Word.

Hold on, *if* you have faith?

In Matthew 17:20, Jesus says if you have faith, you could move mountains. Then He tells you in the next verse (or Mark 9:29) what is needed. *Pray* (remain in me), not 'get permission.' Luke 10:19 says you already have permission (authority). The disciples already had permission too, but their faith was little.

As we become more established (fully persuaded) in the truth of His Word and His character by remaining in Him, dwelling under the shelter of the Most High, and renewing our mind, our actions change. How much we act, is governed by how much we believe – not the quantity, but the conviction. People say they believe Jesus bore the stripes for healing, but will they lay hands?

Faith is strengthened through prayer (remaining)

What do you believe?

We are invited (strongly encouraged) to put into action what we believe, to be doers. God then works with the choices we make – to draw near, remain, submit, resist, love, ask, seek, knock, serve, be humble, and act in faith – to sculpt the future. Romans 8:28, which people love to quote says, He *works* all things together.

> *...that the genuineness of your faith, being much more precious than gold that perishes, though it is tested by fire, may be found to praise, honour, and glory at the revelation of Jesus Christ,*
>
> 1 Peter 1:7

The strength (conviction or genuineness) of our faith, is being able to continue living what we believe when there is resistance. If you believe God is resisting you, submit and sort yourself out; if not, keep standing. Standing is not about being passive. It is not about backing down from God's Word. We want Him to back His Word, but will we?

If you believe we should love, faith is living in a way that is loving. Having little faith is loving only those who love you. Greater faith is being able to love those who persecute you.

Do you believe you are called to cast out devils as per Mark 16:17-18? If you believe that is the case, what does faith look like? Dead faith in that area would mean not even trying. Little faith, as per the disciples in Matthew 17:16, meant that they couldn't do it. Jesus got it done. How can we get it done? By praying, remaining in Him, and renewing our mind. Then we can bear much fruit and prove what is His will.

Make an action?

You can pretend all you want that your actions don't impact the future, and our God will still work with that. But He would much prefer you gave Him something good to work with.

To live by faith is to _action_ what we _believe_, not just make the future something we react to, get out the popcorn, and watch (live by sight). We are to speak to the storm, to speak to the mountain, but also to let God (give Him opportunity) be part of our lives by praying His will be done.

Live by faith, but do it walking with Him

Speaking is one action, but is not the only one. Have you ever heard the saying, "You're so heavenly minded that you're no earthly good?" I believe this saying came about because people were relying on God to do everything instead of living by faith, doing their part, and using what God had put in their hand. In other words, trying to meet needs with seeds, instead of producing fruit.

When we remain in Him, we become better aware of what's _already_ in our hand. The Bible says we have 'all things that pertain to life and godliness' (2 Peter 1:3), but what else do we already have?

> *Now we have received, not the spirit of the world, but the Spirit who is from God, that we might know the things that have been freely given to us by God.*
>
> *1 Corinthians 2:12*

In Christ, we have so much more than a ticket to heaven. What else has been freely given? What I have, give I thee! If we don't know what we have, we will probably be unsuccessful in giving it. Faith is living (action) knowing (believing) what's in our hand when we can't see it there. If we can see it, then it is not faith, it is sight.

Don't wait for sight before you live by faith!

Our Father in heaven loves us regardless of whether we exercise faith – but we are commanded to live by it, not just use it on a rainy day or when facing death. God is love, but the Word says it is impossible to please Him without faith. I know that my Father loves me and I don't need to earn it, but I would love to please Him more if I can. I love my kids, but when I see them doing things like praying for others, it impacts (pleases) me. Grace is that God loved you before you loved Him, but there are fruit and treasures promised to those who remain in Him and are strong, merciful, and make peace, etc.

> *But do you want to know, O foolish man, that faith without works is dead?*
>
> *James 2:20*

When Jesus says, "Your faith has healed you," I personally believe all He was saying was that the action of coming to Him believing they could be made well, got them well. It wasn't the presentation of some sufficient quantity of supernatural currency.

What kind of future do you want?

Imagine looking out your window wanting to see some trees bearing fruit, yet nobody had planted any. So, you roll up your sleeves, get outside, and plant some. The next day you look out your window, the young trees are there, but without fruit. A few months later your neighbour asks you for some fruit, but you have to turn them away empty-handed. Day after day for a few years, you look in anticipation. Finally, fruit starts budding. If you want to have fruit trees in your future, their existence may be a result of a choice you make today.

Faith plants!

Take responsibility to plant a tree today, instead of begging God for a piece of fruit in the future.

The kingdom of God is like a seed that grows. The Bible tells us that the Word is a seed, but not every soil produces a harvest. That needs to sink in. We are responsible to make sure that we are good soil, and that faith (seed, what we believe) comes by hearing the Word of God. Are we listening?

We are God's field, let Him plant

What actions are you taking in faith?

Many want to respond more Christ-like in their interactions with others. This comes from having a stronger relationship with Him, spending time renewing their mind, learning what He would do, and seeing what He did. We do this in the life leading up to those moments. If we want to respond more like Him tomorrow (reap), then we should spend time getting to know Him today (sow).

If you want more peace in your future (reap), then plant seeds today (sow). The fastest way to have more peace in your life is to know God better, setting your mind on Him. Building stronger connections with Him today results in more peace in the future.

People are to be encouraged. God commands us to encourage one another daily (Hebrews 3:13). Overcome evil with good. Are you doing unto others as you would have done unto you? If you want to receive kind words in your future (reap), are you giving kind words today (sow)?

What are some ways we can sow in faith:

- Read the Word
- Pray
- Worship
- Use the gift of tongues
- Give to the poor
- Visit the sick
- Help the orphans and widows
- Encourage those in prison
- Bless those who curse you

- And so much more

A big emphasis in my life recently is a desire to reap healing. What should I sow?

Firstly, I needed to know God's Word about it, that it is something that could be sown. When I discovered that healing was always God's will, then I sought to sow it. Just for your pondering, people who know it is always God's will to heal, tend to be known for ministering it. Even though they don't always see it, they still believe it. Live by faith, not by sight.

In the same way, we don't determine God's willingness to save someone by whether they receive it; we don't determine God's will to heal by whether someone is healed. Jesus still brought healing where the disciples had failed.

Sowing it meant making it happen. Making it happen may sound foreign to you, but the first healing I ministered was a wobbly tooth, and that took praying, pressing, and wrestling many times before it set itself firmly back in place. The person I was praying for went from tears of pain, to tears of joy. That may seem like a small thing, but it was the first time in twenty-five plus years of being a Christian that I had seen someone healed of anything. It was worth fighting the good fight for as it lead to many more healings.

When we realise that God is not resisting us, but rather some weak devil, we become more persevering. I often see people healed after praying multiple times. People seem shocked when I ask to pray again, because they believe I was just being nice, or failing to convince God, but I'm just trying to get the job done (being diligent to believe). God is convinced. Jesus bore the stripes!

There are many things that we can sow in faith today which will shape our future, but people won't take responsibility to sow until they understand it makes a difference.

I really want to stir you to live by faith, which means:

- being intentional in knowing what you believe, and
- letting that determine how you live.

Hope vs Wishing

It's important we talk about hope. The Bible says we should always be ready to give a reason for having it. If someone was drowning in their life, hope as discussed ahead is the lifesaver that I would throw them.

> *But sanctify the Lord God in your hearts, and always be ready to give a defence to everyone who asks you a reason for the hope that is in you, with meekness and fear…*
>
> 1 Peter 3:15

In the Word, we find quite a few mentions of hope. Some that stand out to me are, 'May the God of hope … cause you to abound in hope' (Romans 15:13), 'He has given us new birth again to a living hope' (1 Peter 1:3), and we don't 'sorrow as others who have no hope' (1 Thessalonians 4:13). In the health battle I am in as I write this, hope absolutely is an anchor to my soul (Hebrews 6:19). It is one of the three things that remain (1 Corinthians 13:13). Real hope is one of the most valuable things I could give you.

How much has it cost me that I didn't know some basic truths, like what hope is? It is my desire that sharing how I see it now will give more strength to your whole life, even if you find yourself grieved by various trials.

How would you define hope?

My past definition of hope was: the desire of a preferred outcome from an unknown future. In other words, just wishful thinking. If that was all hope was, how is God the God of it? How does character become it (Romans 5:3-4)? Is wishful thinking really an anchor for my soul?

I feel to start by highlighting that there are two key Greek words that are both translated hope. Not surprisingly they have two different meanings. We find *elpizō* hope used thirty-one times in the King James Version, and *elpis* hope used forty-eight times. This verse uses both, so what's the difference?

> *For we were saved in this hope, but hope that is seen is not hope; for why does one still hope for what he sees?*
>
> *Romans 8:24*

I'm not a Greek expert, but looking at the way different Greek words are used and not just taking translations at face value has allowed God to lead me in some life-altering revelations. In my study of the ones relating to hope, I found that *elpizō* hope is about the preferred outcome from an unknown future, and the other *elpis* hope is longing for the fulfilment of something known. Both are the longing of something not seen (realised), but one is about *knowing* what you will see.

Unknown and known

This immediately made things so much clearer to me. This is the central point of my revelation, that the more we know God (have *elpis* hope), the more we can trust him for unknown things in the future (*elpizō* hope).

You may find it interesting that faith in Hebrews 11:1 is the substance of things unknown (*elpizō* hope), while Romans 15:13 says, 'May the God of hope [*elpis*] fill you with all joy and peace in believing that you may abound in hope [*elpis*]'.

I was recently called a man of great faith, but I would rather be called a man of great hope (*elpis*). The strength of my faith is a by-product of my hope. My knowing God gives me more boldness and confidence in trusting Him. My faith is not some gift that I have been graced with that others don't have. It is a fruit from my increased desire to know Him, abounding as a result of renewing my mind and correcting my believing.

If you want greater faith, get greater hope

Circumstances led me to press into knowing Him more, but you don't need to face the same things I have to increase your hope – it can abound now. Looking back, I would have had so much more strength, peace, faith, and love if I had had more hope going into trials. Hope is no small thing. It can really change how your life goes.

The following, I found, significantly increased my hope.

Point 1:
God loves you (John 3:16)! I really want people to get this point, as wrong believing has so twisted people's definition of love that they believe *everything* that happens in their life is God showing love or 'love in disguise.' Who is described as one who disguises or masquerades (2 Corinthians 11:14)? The better you understand love, the more hope you have in God.

Let your understanding of love (who God is) be without hypocrisy (Romans 12:9). Stop calling evil good and mixing the two. Know what is from God's hand, and what is not.

God is so for you! He wants to give you a hope (Jeremiah 29:11). He desires your future to have the blessings of Abraham. God wants you *sozo* (saved) (1 Timothy 2:4), which is a whole lot more than just receiving a ticket to heaven. 'Greater is He that is in you than he who is in the world'. God is good, loving, compassionate, merciful, kind, faithful, and gives strength to the weary. Jesus came that we might have life.

The picture I previously had of God was developed by the way my life went or the way it had gone for others, instead of believing how the Word describes Him. Like the man who looks in the mirror then walks away and forgets what he looks like, I had closed my Bible and been deceived as to who God was by what I saw in life. Blinded by my sight. The Bible instructs us not to live by sight. God is who He says He is, not who your experiences dictate.

Point 2:

God is sovereign. Excuse me while I go on a tangent here, but understanding this point has so much effect on your hope. Why does this good God allow evil? This is a question people arrive at when they think God is determining everything that happens. God doesn't get everything He wants just because He wants it. God allows choice, not evil.

People use *their* choice to allow evil. The devil is using his choice to convince us what we should allow through ours. If one person goes to hell, God is not getting what He wants. He can do anything, but He is not controlling everything (1 John 5:19). Ask yourself, can I sin? If you don't resist sin until bloodshed and give in, then you can make something happen that God doesn't want.

What if your sin hurts someone else?

At what point do you start blaming God for the results of your choices? 'Do not be deceived ... whatever a man sows, that he will also reap' (Galatians 6:7). Are you blaming God for your sowing and reaping the wrong things, or not sowing and reaping the right (life giving) things? If people believe that God determines everything, they start to ask Him why they didn't reap what they didn't sow, or why they reaped the wrong that they or somebody else sowed. We get to choose!

Choose this day whom you will serve. Choose to serve righteousness. Choose life. Choose to plant what you want to reap. God has the power to do anything, even use my bad choices for good (Romans 8:28).

Knowing there is a difference between what happens, and what God wants to happen, gives me tremendous hope. God tells us to know what is of Him (Ephesians 5:17), which means some things are not. I have hope knowing that the God who can make anything happen is for me. I have hope knowing that just because something is happening doesn't mean that it is of God. Now I can pray confidently, boldly, continually, with hope, "Thy will be done," and stand, persevere, fight the good fight of faith until I see it done.

Once you determine what things are of God, you start to see what is not. If it is God, then it is good. Don't be deceived when it is not (James 1:16-17). Submit to what is God, and resist what isn't. Knowing that you are not resisting God gives you incredible hope, strength, and even joy when you *fall* into hard stuff. You start fighting as a good soldier, overcoming evil with good, on purpose. You become much less tolerant towards sowing the things that don't have a good harvest, thus giving the devil a foothold. You start to become much more intentional about sowing things you do want to reap from.

Point 3:

God is faithful even when we are not (2 Timothy 2:13). I know that at times I have not lived as God desires for me. However, I am not leaning on my faithfulness; I am forgetting what lies behind, and I lean on His. His grace is sufficient; He is strong where I am weak. I am aware there can be a cost when sin abounds, but there is more grace.

Should we go on sinning then?

An important revelation to me was my need to be aware of who I am giving place to. When I sinned, I used to think I was giving room for God to punish me – but Jesus has already borne it all. There are some things God wants us to deal with, e.g. forgiveness, but in sin we are giving opportunity to the devil to steal, kill and destroy, and that's not what I want in my future. Don't give him a foothold.

When we exercise things like prayer, faith, humility, etc., we are giving opportunity to God, and that I do want. It is not about making right and wrong decisions, eating from the wrong tree. It is about life, eating from the life-giving one. Set your mind on what brings life.

In the past I had viewed things like reading the Word as doing the 'right thing'. If I didn't do it, my conscience condemned me, and I would say things like, "I don't read as much as I should." I compare this with eating from the wrong tree. Now I read to bring life. I read to give opportunity to God, to renew my mind, and grow the things I want in my life.

Point 4:

Possibly the most important point when it comes to hope is that God is merciful! We can get so caught up with our ability to do things right that we forget about God. Hebrews 11:6 says that when we approach God, we must believe that He is. Many translations use the word 'exists' in this verse, but my study shows that it is speaking more about knowing His characteristics than His state of being.

> *But without faith it is impossible to please Him, for he who comes to God must believe that He is, and that He is a rewarder of those who diligently seek Him.*
>
> *Hebrews 11:6*

The Word says He is merciful in more instances than you might expect. How we see God, changes how we receive from Him. Just think of the story of the talents. If we view God in the wrong way, it can have big consequences. Do you see a God who gives more to those who are faithful with what they have, or as a harsh master?

Side note: For some reason, many people see God as angry, most likely because they have attributed works of the devil to Him. I had myself, but as I am seeing Him differently now, I am receiving from Him differently. Are people hoping to receive joy? Joyful is not a view of God that comes naturally for me, so I am renewing my mind to see Him that way. Do you see God as being joyful? If joy is a fruit of the Spirit, is God expecting you to become something He isn't? How or why do we think we can become what we do not see Him being? We are supposed to have joy inexpressible (1 Peter 1:8).

We must see Him as He is, not as we reason. (Psalm 16:11, Zephaniah 3:17, Isaiah 62:5).

Point 5:
Believe! All things are possible to Him who believes.

> *Now may the God of hope fill you with all joy and peace in believing, that you may abound in hope by the power of the Holy Spirit.*
>
> *Romans 15:13*

Believing releases hope. See Point 1 – God loves you, He is for you, is all-powerful, and works things for good. Knowing that, gives me hope. In partnership with God our hope can abound. Give Him more opportunity to be in your life.

Hope (*elpis*) is about knowing God, believing and trusting Him, not letting circumstances define who you think He is. The better you know God, the more hope you have. Abounding in hope is a result of believing.

Love and Hate

Has it ever crossed your mind that out of all the things God could desire from us, He chooses our love? Then He tells us to love others, as well. Surely, I was going to do this anyway? Wasn't I?

In a moment of frustration with how my body was acting (fighting sickness), I asked God in anger what He even cared about, and I believe He quickly replied, "Love!" In hindsight it seems obvious. I mean, isn't love the basis of the first and second greatest commandments? In the story of Job, we see how much the devil threw at him to try and stop him loving God. Regardless of what life (or the devil) throws your way, will you still love?

What is love?

Sometimes God responds so quickly it almost startles you. I wonder if He gets excited when people ask Him certain things. I asked God why He loves me, and I believe He answered, "Why love anybody?" This response started some rather deep thinking for me. I'd never asked that question before. I thought about how my kids did not have to do anything to earn my love – but be my kids. They have challenged my ability to act in love at times. However, these moments weren't about deciding if they were worth loving. Rather, they were exposing holes in my character.

Are you aware that right now you are loved by God? He so loves us that He sent His Son to die for us, including the very people nailing Jesus to the Cross. This is how we know what love is… God loved us before we had done a single thing to receive it. Should we have the same attitude?

> *He who does not love does not know God, for God is love.*
>
> 1 John 4:8

Love is who God is, not what He decides to do. If we interact with God, we get loved. This is not because of a choice He makes, but the mere fact we are in the presence of Love. This understanding led me to realise that this type of love is not dependent on a decision, but is a result (a fruit) of who we are. We do it because that is what we're made of.

You may not like the fact that you can't make God love you more, but you should be over the moon that you can't make Him love you less. He is not changing His nature based on your performance.

To me, there are two parts to love:

Firstly, God is love, and Scripture says in 2 Corinthians 5:18 we are made of God. We are made of love; it is our new nature. When you are born again, your spirit is made a new creation, but your soul needs renewing to live accordingly.

We are the righteousness of God in Christ Jesus (our nature when born again), but the way people think is causing them not to act like it at times. Just because you do or don't act like something, doesn't change your nature. I can act like some kind of animal all I want, but that doesn't make me one.

Secondly, we are to put on! I believe this is the difference between who I am (nature), and how I currently act by default (percentage of my mind renewed). Therefore, as the new man, put on love – not as a thistle bush trying to bear figs, but as a fig tree bears figs. Love is the fruit of your new nature. As we correct our thinking, we will have less to put on. We are not trying to become something we are not; we are pressing and reaching to live as we are, who we have been newly created in Christ.

A friend of mine gave me a great way to picture this, which I have slightly adapted. Imagine living for many years as a beggar, then finding out you were snatched from a palace as an infant and were now about to become a king. You might have to learn how one acts (look in the Word as in a mirror), and 'put on' how a king acts while your mind is being renewed. We are kings and priests (identity) (Revelation 1:6), but it has been given to us to choose how much we live like one (actions).

Why are some people so hard to love?

Some people make it hard to receive love from God. Not because they are any worse than the ones who pierced His Son, but because they refuse to come to Him. I believe this is a major reason we are to go into all the world and bring the kingdom near to people. We are to bring love (God) to people, to love our neighbour, love those we deem our enemies. To be salt and light, that people will see Christ in us and praise God and ask about the hope we have. Not to be a hypocrite and fake who we aren't, but to be who we are around them, manifesting love to the extent that Christ is formed in our hearts. Who we are is not dependent on the person standing in front of us.

Not love <u>does</u>, but love <u>is</u>!

A key revelation for me was that love *is*, not love *does* (1 Corinthians 13). I am renewing my mind to be who God made me, not to act well based on my circumstances. My ability to love reflects me, not you. I know when I don't act in a loving way, it is a lack of a fruit. This fruit grows from being connected to the vine, knowing God – not some failed action to focus on. Though it may help to know how love is described, like a way to measure it (love is patient, love is kind, etc.), our main pursuit is knowing Him, and knowing who we are in Christ – and that should produce the fruit of love in us.

Where does hate fit in?

In my trying to understand love, I felt led to understand hate. It seems strange to focus on that when we are supposed to dwell on good. It may take you by surprise, but the fear of the Lord is to *hate* evil (Proverbs 8:13), and the fear of the Lord is the beginning of wisdom (Proverbs 9:10). We are to *hate* evil (Romans 12:9, Psalms 97:10, Amos 5:15).

God is not telling you to spend time focussing on (dwelling on, meditating on) evil but is instructing you to hate it. Be simple about evil, but hate it (Romans 16:19)

> *Let love be without hypocrisy. Abhor what is evil. Cling to what is good.*
>
> *Romans 12:9*

For me to properly understand what love is (who God is), I must be able to recognise and abhor what is evil. Many people seem uncomfortable with the concept of hate. I think this is because it is largely viewed as a negative thing that hurts people. However, when you take people out of the equation, this can lead to a righteous hate of things like evil. There are many things I hate, and most of them could be described as love not in operation.

When you understand hate as something bad then focussing on it is wrong, but I began to see that hate and love are at times the same thing. God loves truth and hates lies – it is the same. Jesus went about doing good and healing all, and at the same time was destroying the works of the enemy. Different sides of the same coin. Hate directed correctly can actually be loving toward its opposite. We are not to hate people, but we should hate them being oppressed, and this should manifest in us doing something, which will likely look like love. Love should motivate us, but at times while we are learning to love genuinely, we can be motivated by hate of evil.

Love is not an emotion, it is shown in action. I feel somewhat uncomfortable saying this, and some reading it may feel this way too, but I love you. If you came into my house, I would act in a way that would be loving to you. I wouldn't just sit there and have some feeling. I would offer you a drink and/or something to eat. I would make sure it wasn't too hot or cold. I would ask you how you were and pray or speak in faith for God's will to be more abundant in your life.

Jesus so loves you right now and you haven't done a thing to earn it. But just as you have to be in my presence for me to offer you a drink, we need to come to Jesus to receive from Him. We must sit at his feet, give him our attention, and walk with Him. It is hard to hear from Him when you are binge-watching a TV series, blasting your favourite album, or stuck in the latest game. In the natural you probably wouldn't be happy for me to talk to you the whole time a movie was playing. Make room in your life where He is given the chance to speak.

The Father gives us a commandment to love people. To obey that commandment, I must act in love toward you whether I want to or not. With some people I have more feelings to overcome, more buttons they press, more flaws in my character which they somehow exploit, and it takes more effort to allow love for them, but that is what I am called to do. If more effort is required, then more effort is given. Put on love.

You are loved!

Hate is not an emotion either, it is an action. It's not just a feeling of hate. Some things leave a bad taste in your mouth, but unless you are driven to action about them, then really, you just don't like them.

A big issue I see in the body of Christ at the moment is that people are trying to love good, but refuse to hate evil, and so their love gets distorted (is not genuine), and is just viewed as niceness, not kindness. For example, if people love righteousness but don't hate sin, it only makes them feel guilty occasionally, so they tolerate it, say they are praying about it, may get others to pray too, and 'struggle' with it. Speaking from my own experience, when I started hating sin/evil, I stopped giving it a foothold.

We rightly celebrate a person's victory of overcoming temptation, but if it gets the better of them, we pat them on the back and say, "Better luck next time." We are to love people, to set them free, to act against sin trying to oppress them. That might look like healing, deliverance or discipleship, but our level of hate towards the sin, sickness or oppression will affect our action of love towards people.

The more we hate the wrong, the more we act in love towards the right. We should be motivated by love, but that gets compromised (not genuine) when we refuse to hate evil. Abhor (hate) what is evil.

I am growing in my hatred of sickness, which means I am more willing to pray for healing, which means I am seeing more healed, which means I am getting less tolerant toward it afflicting people. The more I hate it, the more persistence I have to act against it. Yes, I am learning to resist sickness in my love for people, but not having hated it previously has stopped me from acting. There is so much sickness around, but do you hate it enough to even lay your hands?

It is the same with deliverance. Hating that some people are being influenced or bound by the kingdom of darkness means that I am more willing to pray with people and cast out devils, as per Mark 16:17-18.

Can we speak the truth in love?

We live in a culture where telling the truth could be classed as hate speech. When is it loving to tell someone that sugary sodas, pies and doughnuts every day is not a healthy diet? Do we say it before or after it causes them health issues like obesity, heart attacks, high blood pressure, diabetes, etc.? Through God anything can be overcome, but people are allowing unnecessary obstacles in the name of niceness, a mere attempt to love without truth.

There are probably not a lot of comfortable situations in which we can talk to someone about their diet, financial choices, addictions, beliefs about God, etc., but I would rather you thought less of me, than having to watch you go through some unnecessary hardship or attend an early funeral.

I would say that many times love is hindered because of a fear of man (feelings). God is love, and we are supposed have more fear of God (reverence, higher commitment to) than man. My desire to love you is much stronger than my desire to be liked by you.

If people believe that God is choosing for everything to happen, then the most disgusting of things are somehow seen as loving because 'they're from God'. But if I did those same things, people might try to take my life. How am I supposed to be growing in my intimacy with God if I am not allowed to do what I see the Father doing, the things He is blamed for? The truth is that some things are not Him (not love) and should not be repeated. Know what is of Him.

Anointing and Authority

What is an anointing, and do we need one? If so, how do we get one, assuming we even have a say about it? What is a manifestation of Holy Spirit, and what is a fruit of someone who believes? Is the likelihood of God's will occurring, dependant on getting Holy Spirit to show up sufficiently, or is it only from His will when He shows up and acts? If we can get more of Holy Spirit at our will, how do we do that? Is being anointed a valid reason for why someone can do something or why someone else can't? These are some great questions if you are seeking to understand why a promise of God is not manifesting.

My reason for bringing this subject up is that I believe needing an anointing can be used as an excuse (weight, hindrance, or stronghold) for people to explain away their failure to accomplish something. More importantly, it is used to justify not pressing and reaching, like the Scriptures instruct (Philippians 3:13, Hebrews 6:12, 2 Corinthians 12:12, Colossians 1:11, 2 Peter 1:5-8).

Although these explanations may be used to comfort, they are far from biblical, and their tradition (passed on reasoning) is stopping the church from living in truth (God's Word) and having victory. I want you to inherit God's promises, not be persuaded with some carefully crafted reasoning.

Hear me again, it is not important that you believe what I believe, but that you know what you believe, that it is the truth, and it makes you free. Faith is the action of your belief, which is hard to have when you don't know what that is.

Based on my study, the definition of anointing is simply the act of setting apart or consecrating someone or something for a specific purpose, often done in the Bible through the application of oil.

Anointing means given purpose. You were given purpose.

Every time we are commanded to do something in the Word of God, we are anointed to do that thing. Do you know the purposes you have been given? According to the Word in Matthew 28:16-28, the disciples of Jesus were told to teach their disciples to follow all they were commanded to do. What were they told to do that you are excluded from?

What you have been anointed to do is not determined by whether you succeed at it. Whether something is seemingly impossible or not, does not excuse you from doing it. Imagine for a moment I asked you to do something as simple as get me a glass of water. Do you question if you are anointed for the job because you aren't sure where my cups are? Or do you learn what is needed to get the job done? If the water takes a while to come out of the tap, do you persevere, or tell me it's too hard and I can't have what I want? Whether you fail to deliver does not mean I didn't ask. If God were to ask people why they didn't deliver/buried their talent/followed their feeling/ignored His instructions, what will they say? That they thought He was being harsh expecting people to make good on what He invested? God invested His Son.

Is God 'hot' about this?

One very helpful revelation I had which I think is worth your serious consideration, is how God is so black-and-white on issues. If a verse seems to put Him in the grey on something, it is usually because it is not understood. If God needed you to get an anointing (special ability) to do His will, it would be in your Bible frequently, but it's not.

There are only a couple of verses that might be interpreted that way, often by those who want the Bible to justify their beliefs. Most debate I have on doctrine or theology is when people are trying to put God in the grey. There is no shadow of turning with Him, no variableness (James 1:17). He is either hot or cold, and He vomits the lukewarm out of His mouth (Revelation 3:15-16). Don't make a doctrine for yourself that nullifies the Word and power of God.

Don't judge God by what experience says, judge experience by what God says

Let's assume for a moment that to be anointed does mean to have special abilities to do specific things. What are some verses that say I am *not* limited by not having an anointing.

- Philippians 4:13 – 'I can do all things through Christ who strengthens me.' Well, there's one.
- Mark 9:23 – 'Jesus said to him, "If you can believe, all things are possible to him who believes." Two.
- Ephesians 4:15 – '…but, speaking the truth in love, may grow up in all things into Him who is the head—Christ…' Three.
- 1 John 4:17 – '…because as He is, so are we in this world.; People say, "But I'm not Jesus." There was nothing He failed at. Four.
- John 14:12 – '…he who believes in Me, the works that I do he will do also…' What did Jesus do? Five.

There are probably other verses I could use, but imagine if any of these were followed by '…with the right anointing.' Let's do the opposite. What are the verses saying I am limited by not having an anointing? None.

You may point out here that we need Holy Spirit to manifest the gifts of Holy Spirit, and you would be right. However, these are as He wills, not as you are anointed.

Jesus being our example, what anointing did He have?

A few Scriptures describe why Jesus came to earth. He definitely had a purpose, but what special abilities did He possess? Regardless of what you think they are, if you believe in Him, you can do the same, and greater (John 14:12). We are to grow in Him in all things.

He told the twelve to heal the sick and cast out devils, etc., and then told the seventy to do the same. Other people who didn't even have relationship with Jesus were accomplishing things (Mark 9:38, Matthew 7:22-23). Elders (experienced, not positional) can heal the sick (James 5:14-15). Jesus said that believers could do the same works as Him. Did He tell anybody to get an anointing?

Some people refer to the gift that was in Timothy, through prophecy and the laying on of hands, as an anointing. What, according to the Bible, is given by the laying on of hands? The answer is Holy Spirit (Acts 19:6) or appointment to ministry (1 Timothy 5:22).

It is going into the grey to say that Timothy was the only person in the New Covenant with an anointing (special ability) given to him. 2 Timothy 1:6 refers to the gift in him, and the next verse says God has given a spirit (of power, love, and a sound mind), not an ability. Paul blessed Timothy for Timothy's sake. Acts 1:8 – the Spirit of the Lord is on us (given/received) to be a witness, not *to* witness. Holy Spirit is not on people to help them be fake and disguise who they aren't, but to help them shine the light of Christ in them.

Is the Holy Spirit our anointing?

This is such an important question to answer. Is it only God's will that determines when Holy Spirit shows up and grants us our requests? Or do we sometimes need to fight the good fight and persevere to possess His promises?

Mathew 3:16 says the Spirit of God descended on Him like a dove, and we find in Luke 4:18 Jesus saying, '"The Spirit of the Lord is upon Me because He has anointed Me..."' Acts 10:38 describes how God anointed Jesus of Nazareth with the Holy Spirit. The Holy Spirit wasn't the anointing, Holy Spirit was given *with* the anointing, to help Jesus with His anointing.

Holy Spirit is our helper, not the anointing

If you don't have Holy Spirit (Acts 19:2), you still have been given a purpose (an anointing), but having Holy Spirit will help you with your purpose. Jesus was given Holy Spirit because He was anointed. I hear some asking, "Wasn't He also given power?" We'll come back to that.

Like Jesus, we should seek to get ourselves baptised in Holy Spirit (John 20:22, John 16:7). We are to imitate Paul as he imitates Christ, and be filled with Holy Spirit (Ephesians 5:18). What about the other disciples? Partner with Holy Spirit! (Acts 2:38). Holy Spirit helps us carry out our anointing. The Bible is pretty clear, we should get Holy Spirit.

If you fail, is it because you lack anointing?

The disciples said, "Why could we not do it?" The answer was to correct their believing, not to get an anointing. There is more available to us when we believe correctly, and we can get ourselves into a position where we can cast demons out, etc. But will we count the cost and pay the price? Let Christ be fully formed in your hearts. Like a toddler entering the room, the whole person is there, but they will likely need some forming before they can shift a bookcase.

If you have faith, not if you have anointing

People can go astray thinking that different giftings and talents are anointings. We are members of a body and we each have various things that we are good at, enjoy doing, find easy, are graced to do, or areas where we are more closely following Holy Spirit. I wouldn't ask my friend who bakes the best brownies to build me a shed, any more than I would call on my friend who is a builder to fix my computer. People can do all things, but if I know someone skilled in an area, I'd go to them first. Some people seem to have a superpower with spreadsheets and others hitting a nail into wood, but these are abilities, not anointings.

When we look at the five-fold ministry, it is grace (things found easier) and strength that is given to help build the church and equip us for doing the work, not to do the work for us. To help grow us into a perfect man. God graced people to build us up so we can better fulfil our purpose, our anointing.

I have friends who have faith for God to provide financially, but I would be less likely to call on them if I needed healing. They know God more as Jehovah Jireh (their minds have been renewed in this area) than Jehovah Rapha. If they were the only people available to me, Holy Spirit can give them the faith they need or distribute a gift of healing as He wills. There are attributes of God we have tasted and seen, and attributes we have not. I have seen a lot of backs healed and so I find it easier to have faith for that, but there are illnesses I haven't seen healed yet. I pray fervently for breakthroughs knowing that a healing should happen according to His Word regardless of whether my eyes have seen it, but I find it harder to expect. Live by faith, not by sight. I know I can get myself to a place (develop my character) where I can, so I press and reach, not comfort myself with some excuse like needing an anointing.

What about power?

Let's start with this verse, '..."Not by might nor by power, but by My Spirit," says the Lord...' (Zechariah 4:6). We have been given a Spirit of power (2 Timothy 1:7). The same Spirit (or power, as in some translations) that rose Christ from the dead lives in us (Romans 8:11). I can't imagine that you need more power than that which raised to life someone who had been marred more than any man and been dead for three days, but it seems you have that. Peter and John made a lame man walk and didn't give any credit to power, but to the name of Jesus! How many verses are directing you to get power?

> **Anointing means purpose, not ability**

Authority

Jesus gave us authority when he commanded us to do something that needs power. He would not tell you to carry out a task you weren't able to do. Please let this sink in, but just because something is possible (within the realm of achievable), doesn't mean that you can do it. Likewise, just because you can't do it, doesn't mean you couldn't.

Holy Spirit is not the authority, but helps us exercise the authority already given us (1 Corinthians 2:12).

> **Authority is the given right to use power**

Have we got the right?

There are a few ways we could discuss authority. I want to focus on what God has given believers, or representatives, of His kingdom. I am not talking about authority over others, but exercising authority over the kingdom of darkness as per Luke 10:19.

For us to have this kind of authority, a person who already has the authority must delegate it to us. Jesus said, "All authority in heaven and on earth has been given to Me, therefore go! I give [delegate] to you authority to get my will accomplished. Cast out devils, heal the sick, cleanse lepers, raise the dead, preach the kingdom. Whatever you bind on earth will be bound in heaven, whatever you loose, will be loosed." According to Scripture we have been given authority, but many will question this by whether their prayers are answered.

Do we have authority only in our victories, or are we at times simply unsuccessful in enforcing the authority we have?

We need to understand that God is not controlling everything, and that He doesn't always get what He wants. If you do wrong or fail to do right, it is sin and God is not getting what He wants. We can fail to minister the kingdom at times God wants us to.

> *Therefore, do not be unwise, but understand what the will of the Lord is.*
>
> *Ephesians 5:17*

Some things are clearly not the will of the Lord! Once you understand that, the Bible and your faith will come alive. So many things have happened that were not decided by God. Whether or not we receive what we are praying for, does not mean God chose its outcome. The biggest deception I find regarding authority is that when something is resisted, people think it is not approved by God. People have confused what is of God, with what is not, because they think God is choosing everything.

Why could we not cast it out?

There are two types of resistance:

- from the kingdom of God
- from the kingdom of darkness

Just because we couldn't do it, doesn't necessarily mean the resistance came from God, but it may have.

There are several things that God resists, e.g. the proud (1 Peter 5:5), unforgiveness (Matthew 18:34-35), the carnal mind (Romans 8:7), friendship with the world (James 4:4), disunity in marriage (1 Peter 3:7), being lukewarm (Revelation 3:16), etc. But if these things are in play, you will probably know. Ask God to bring these to light as you walk with Him. They are not about praying (ministering) right, but to do with living right.

> *But he who sins against me wrongs his own soul; All those who hate me love death.*
>
> *Proverbs 8:36*

When we don't operate (run) within the rules (spiritual laws, policies) of the kingdom we represent, it is like having our punches pulled, trying to swing with a dislocated shoulder, or being one who beats the air. When we don't run according to the rules, we can't expect to win the prize. I'm not talking about getting to heaven, I am referring to being able to manifest heaven on earth. Are you taking responsibility for the effectiveness of your prayers? How hard do you punch? Athletes must live in a certain way (discipline their body) to excel in the sport they have chosen. Are you choosing to be disciplined in running your race well?

Find out how God wants you to run. There are ways your prayers can be more effective – find out how. Those who represent His kingdom well carry effective weapons. Are you swinging with a wooden sword or a blunt axe (Ecclesiastes 10:10) and hoping to be as effective as those swinging a sharpened weapon?

God resists the proud, not giving the kingdom

When it is clear God is not resisting you, you need to be aware when the devil is. Don't be unaware of his schemes. The devil is roaming about seeking who he is stronger than, can get an advantage over, is not wearing the right armour, and who will surrender and give him place. Be strong, develop your character, let Christ be fully formed in your heart, and add to your faith. The devil is not stronger than God, but can he devour you?

Some people have concluded that *we* can resist, but the devil can't. Jesus has won the victory over the enemy, but He hopes to see him crushed under our feet too. Jesus's character was not something the devil could find a foothold in and get on top of. Although he certainly tried, there was nothing in Him the devil could use to step up on and lord over Him. Like a climbing wall, the devil can't climb where he has nowhere to grab. Are there areas in your life which will allow the devil to gain the upper hand, that are wrongfully submitted? The Bible commands us to be strong, but who decides if you are? Our resisting and wrestling means there is strength in the opponent to conquer.

> *For we do not wrestle against flesh and blood, but against principalities, against powers, against the rulers of the darkness of this age, against spiritual hosts of wickedness in the heavenly places.*
>
> Ephesians 6:12

If we were to unfortunately lose, who would be responsible for our defeat? God, or the way we are running our race? Hasn't God told us to be strong and to develop our character?

> *…but imitate those who through faith and patience inherit the promises.*
>
> Hebrews 6:12

Many translations of this verse use a different word for 'patience', but they all mean be prepared to contend for the promises. Press and reach, fight the good fight, persevere, endure, stand. Like the Promised Land to the Israelites, it has been provided but it needs to be possessed. Just because it may be challenged, does not mean it is not yours.

> *Truly the signs of an apostle were accomplished among you with all perseverance, in signs and wonders and mighty deeds.*
>
> 2 Corinthians 12:12

Please note the word perseverance (*hypomonē* in the Greek). We are to run our race with it and add it to our faith.

The kingdom of darkness has to put someone in the ring to wrestle with you. The devil is not omnipresent, so his kingdom must have strategies in place depending on who their opponent is. Depending on how much they want to win the fight will determine who is put in the ring. The devil doesn't want to lose any more than you do. The kingdom of darkness is no match for someone who is strong from the kingdom of light, so they must scheme.

The stronger you are than your opposer, the quicker they will admit defeat. This is why James 5:14 instructs you to call for the elders. Tag team and get someone else in on the fight. Not someone who has a better grip on God's ear, but someone who is bigger (in the spirit) and can fight better than you can.

Bigger means that Christ is more formed in their hearts, they have spent more time renewing their mind, they are more fully persuaded, they have tested their faith, and have developed their character. They have been diligent to believe and enter His rest.

In many cases, the devil needs only to resist one prayer, and he's won. Some people immediately reason that their failure was God's decision, instead of realising their own hits might not have been as hard as they could be. Jesus, our example, was as big in the spirit as they come. One move (one prayer) from Him was too much for the enemy to stand. He delivered a one-hit knockout. Smith Wigglesworth said that his own inner man was a thousand times bigger than his outer man. How much power is working in you?

> *Now to Him who is able to do exceedingly abundantly above all that we ask or think, according to the power that works in us...*
>
> *Ephesians 3:20*

Able to – as in, it is possible. It might take us a few moves to inflict the same impact as Christ would have, depending on how much power is working in us. It is not likely that we are as strong as Jesus yet, but we are to grow into Him in all things. If our strength is only just sufficient to overcome the enemy, then all we need do is wear our opponent out, use patience and perseverance, and stand.

> *...strengthened with all might, according to His glorious power, for all patience and longsuffering with joy...*
>
> *Colossians 1:11*

I find it interesting that God strengthens us to persevere, not gives us more authority to manifest the kingdom as He desires.

Your authority doesn't waver, but your strength to use it can

What do we have authority over?

When we accept that what we have authority over is not determined by what we have victory in but what we have been commanded to do, then it is important for us to know what we have authority over.

I point again to Luke 10:19, "'Behold I give you [delegate] authority over all the power of the enemy.'" In many cases, people have determined their authority by what comes without resistance. But what is a work of the enemy, and not a will of God? This stops people in their tracks who have previously believed that anything that happened was a loving work of a God in control. When you accept that some things are not of God, it becomes surprisingly simple.

- Is it in heaven?
- Did Christ do it?
- Did the disciples do it?
- Would you do it?

As in heaven

Pray His will be done and His kingdom come on earth as it is in heaven. Is there sickness in heaven? Pain, oppression, death, poverty, fear, anxiety, depression? If you know it's not in heaven, pray it stops on earth. Not once nicely, but until it changes (be diligent). Pray without ceasing, fervently, keep asking, test your faith and persevere in it, be strong, stand, and do not let the enemy prosper or prevail. Overcome the enemy; conquer and get victory. Prayer doesn't just mean use words. Don't just say, "Be warm and well fed," but do what you know is in your power to do. 'What I have, give I thee.' God being able to do more than we can imagine, is not saying we shouldn't do what we can. But don't just do good without giving God opportunity.

As Christ

God is so often blamed for stuff that Christ never did. The Word says that Jesus is the exact representation of God; in Him all the fullness of God dwells; Jesus and the Father are one; if you've seen Jesus, you've seen the Father. If you can't see Jesus doing it, then you can't see God doing it, and it should be resisted. Did Jesus give someone sickness? God and Christ are one, not a kingdom divided.

As disciples

The great commission (Matthew 28:20) says to teach them to do all they were commanded. The disciples were to teach their disciples, who in turn teach their disciples, who teach their disciples, and on and on until Jesus comes back. What did Jesus tell His disciples to do?

As a good father

"'If you being evil know how to give good gifts...'" (Matthew 7:11) shows us that if we wouldn't do it, we're to stop thinking we're better than God and that He would. There are times when God is involved and if we are not listening to Him, we will see it negatively and mistakenly resist Him. If it is God though, it is good. If in doubt, we're to resist until we know better. God is much more forgiving than the devil.

How does Holy Spirit help?

Luke 10:19 is given to the believer. Jesus commanded believers to heal the sick, which means you can, just by laying hands believing. But a gift of healing from Holy Spirit (present, not ability) can get the job done in a matter of seconds where it might have taken hours standing, pressing and reaching. We are told to cast out devils, and I have heard of people spending a long time to accomplish it where a word of knowledge from Holy Spirit revealing the devil's right to be there, would have done it in no time at all.

He is in your corner and wants to see you win. Seek His advice, let him counsel you. He knows the enemy's weakness, but will you give Him opportunity to tell you? He raised Jesus back to life and He is with, in, and for you.

Anointing means being given purpose, and if that anointing requires power, then authority comes with it. You have been anointed (given purpose) and given authority by the One who has all authority.

Pursuing Peace

I thought I had a pretty good handle on peace, but the more I looked, the less I knew. It passed my understanding, I couldn't get a grip on it, and maybe I was deceived (or ignorant) about what I thought I knew.

To get the most out of this chapter, I recommend having a basic understanding of a Venn diagram. Simply put, it is a way to see how things relate using overlapping shapes, typically circles. Each circle represents something different, for instance animals that are birds, or animals that can swim. Where the circles overlap, it shows things that belong to both groups, e.g. ducks and penguins. It helps us see how things are similar or different.

> *But He was wounded for our transgressions,*
> *He was bruised for our iniquities; The*
> *chastisement for our peace was upon Him, And*
> *by His stripes we are healed.*
>
> Isaiah 53:5

This is a verse I don't often hear discussed outside of healing, but it was so important to God for us to have peace that it is listed among the things Christ gave His life for. I would go as far to say that peace in your soul is of more value than health in your body.

To give more depth to that statement, I personally am being challenged in my body as I write this, but having peace in my soul means that I am pressing and reaching to love and give life. There are others who have thrown away healthy bodies because they couldn't find peace in their souls. So many need healing, but there are just as many, if not more, who lack peace.

Are you wanting more peace?

If so, do you know what you want more of?

How does the Bible define peace?

Before we start, if I were to tell you what peace is, we are likely to disagree. Most people I have talked with have differing opinions on this. In the King James Version, there are a massive four hundred verses containing the English word peace, a hundred-and-four of them in the New Testament. Surely, we can understand it, right? With that many references, should we even have an opinion?

Here lies the challenge: I can't point you to a Scripture and say that this is the definition of peace, for the Bible tells me so. I don't think anyone can. There is no 'peace is' verse or chapter.

In trying to understand peace, I discovered there are two separate questions:

- What is peace?
- What does peace feel like?

When you're not trying to account for feelings, peace is reasonably easy to describe, I think. Discussing how it feels takes more work. The feeling of peace is where people tend to focus their attention, prayers, and questions, but for this next part I want you to put that (the by-product) aside and focus on what gives the feeling.

Peace is being one

That is a big statement worth some exploring.

> *For He Himself is our peace, who has made both one, and has broken down the middle wall of separation…*
>
> *Ephesians 2:14*

I think this is the closest verse you will get to the description of peace, but there is one thing worth highlighting that makes it so much clearer. The start of that verse says, 'For He Himself is *our* peace', not that He was the *only* peace. In another verse we find, '"My peace I leave you, not as the world gives do I give…"' (John 14:27). There is peace God gives, and peace the world gives, but they do not have the same fruit (experience/feeling). Our understanding of our spirit being one with Christ's (renewing our mind) is the peace we want, but it's not the only peace there is. When you take that part of the verse away, you are left with peace being one.

> *"...that they all may be one, as You, Father, are in Me, and I in You; that they also may be one in Us, that the world may believe that You sent Me."*
>
> *John 17:21*

Our spirit, who we are, the born-again new creation, has peace and becomes one with God (Romans 5:1). If you were to represent this in a Venn diagram, there would be just one circle. This does not ever vary. But the place where we experience peace (knowing/feeling) is in our soul, and this overlap can change.

Just like so many things in Scripture, the new creation is, or has them. We are made of God, righteous, blessed with all spiritual blessing, have all things that pertain to life and godliness, and as He is, so are we in this world. These things are given to our spirit (who we are), but our soul (mind, will, emotions) is in the process of being renewed to manifest (experience) them on earth.

> *For to be carnally minded is death, but to be spiritually minded is life and peace.*
>
> *Romans 8:6*

The mind (soul) set on, one with, placed upon, overlapping the spirit, experiences peace. Learning there was a difference between soul and spirit changed my life. Unless your spirit and soul are one, there is more available to you. There are some good teachings on spirit, soul, and body (1 Thess.

5:23), but for now think of the spirit as the born-again, incorruptible new creation, and the soul as where the mind that can be renewed dwells.

Imagine another diagram, where the area the circle representing your soul overlaps with the circle representing your spirit, are one. This would illustrate how much peace with God you *experience*. This is not how much peace you have with God, but what you experience.

Peace with God is not the only peace (being one) we can experience, but it is by far the best available. The key difference I see with God's peace when compared with any other peace found in the world, is that it will never be taken away, and there is no fear or anxiety attached. It's like having the assurance of building your house on the Rock. We ourselves can move away from experiencing it (reduce the overlap), but God will never move. Every other peace (oneness) outside God, comes with fear or anxiety of it being taken away or lost. There are varying levels of confidence that things won't change, but it's never one hundred percent. The less confidant you are, the less peace (feeling) you have.

Peace is a fruit that grows, not a feeling that goes

I think there are two key reasons many don't experience peace today. One is focussing on, praying for, or looking for ways to experience the feeling without understanding where the feeling comes from. The second reason is focussing on making peace (being united to, one with) the world outside of God, instead of making it priority to be one with God (soul overlapping spirit). This adds anxiety to our life, like building on the sand. You can do it, but will it stand when encountering a storm?

We are called to be in the world, but not of it (John 17:14-16). Being of the world is like having a circle that represents who you are, overlapped with anything imaginable, e.g. employment, hobbies, health, fame. Being in the world but not of it is like having a circle that represents who you are, but it only touches other circles and doesn't overlap with them. You can be part of many things, but when they define who you are (are part of you), then you should question if they are in God.

I can mow someone's lawns out of love for them (circles touching), but if I start defining who I am as a landscaper (circles overlapping), that is when I need to be talking with God. You can have peace (be one) with people and things, but if it is outside of God, you have peace that can be experienced as something to lose. If it is in God and gets taken away, you haven't lost any peace (three circles) as the overlap is maintained by Him.

> *...and the peace of God, which surpasses all understanding, will guard your hearts and minds through Christ Jesus.*
>
> *Philippians 4:7*

If God is your financial provider, how provision happens does not matter so much, but if you believe your provision comes from your employment (circles overlapping outside

God) and that is taken away, you lose your peace. Do you look to God to provide? Or to your job?

We are to be one with our spouse, but if we try to do this outside of God, we only have peace where we agree, along with anxiety regarding whether that oneness can be maintained. If this relationship is in God, then our peace (overlap) is maintained by God, and we can experience peace though we go through hard stuff. I am not for a second saying that hard stuff won't be hard – Jesus wept, and there has been many a martyr – but I am saying we can have peace when going through trials.

Christ said the devil had nothing in Him. There were no overlapping circles from the world that were outside God, and He is called the Prince of Peace. Nothing could be used to control, manipulate, or sway Him. His soul was completely one with His spirit, which was one with God. This is what Jesus was praying for us in John 17:21. Once you are born again, your spirit is one with God, but He has left it to us how much we make our *soul* one with them.

Putting the definition of peace to the side, some important points to consider are:

- God wants peace with you, for you, and for you to have it with others (John 16:33, John 14:27, Matthew 5:9).
- The chastisement of our peace was upon Him (Isaiah 53:5).
- It was made available through the Cross (Colossians 1:20).

- One of the first things you receive with salvation is peace (Romans 5:1).
- The Lord blesses His people with peace (Psalms 29:11).
- A fruit of the spirit is peace (Galatians 5:22).
- He will keep in perfect peace those whose minds are stayed on Him (Isaiah 26:3).

I believe God wants us to be in one hundred percent peace, one hundred percent of the time. That doesn't mean we are, it just means we can be.

Do you have peace right now?

Many will pray for peace to overcome fear, anxiety and worry, like it is something that comes and goes. Although at times God can temporarily change the effect of the world's pull on us, the goal is to be one with God completely. It really is the same as giving a man a fish versus teaching a man to fish. God can give you peace, you can be blessed with it, but He wants you to know how to have it all the time.

The Feeling

What does peace feel like?

The best description I can offer for the feeling of peace is that it is the opposite of being in tension. I am not trying to define peace here, but rather how it feels.

It is not just the absence of tension (being pulled in two different directions) but its opposite. How do you put that in words?

It is not just something that is not negative; it is positive. Jesus was tempted in every way we are (pulled) but He remained without sin. He is called the Prince of Peace. Peace is not 'being without pull', but is found or caused by being more submitted to the Spirit than to our flesh. Once again, the mind set on the Spirit is peace.

The most comprehendible picture I can think of is when you know you are being pulled by a steel chain, but it feels like a weak rubber band.

If you want to feel more peace, get more peace

The quickest and best way to have more of the feeling of peace in your life, is to use more of your resources (time, strength), setting your mind on Him, seeking first and remaining in Him. When you apply more of your resources to building the right connection, you have less available for building the wrong ones.

Think of it like giving strength to one side of a tug of war. Who you give strength to will win. If God wins, you get peace. I want more of that.

What creates tension in your life?

This world tries hard to pull our soul (mind) towards being carnal (not evil, but driven by senses, which leads to evil), giving priority to overlapping the flesh instead of the spirit. This 'pull' creates tension that can rob us of the peace (overlap) Christ paid for, if we allow it to shift our focus. Peace has been provided, now it is our job to be diligent to receive it. We have influence on how much our soul and spirit are one (overlap) towards having life and peace as a result. The more they are one, the less we feel the pull of the world.

> *For to be carnally minded is death, but to be spiritually minded is life and peace.*
>
> *Romans 8:6*

The more important something is to you, the more you are tethered (attached) to it. For example, if you really love to sing, then you are tethered to your ability to produce vocal sound. If it were a hobby, you would be more lightly tethered than if it were your employment. The more important it is to you the stronger the connection is. Now imagine your ability to sing was jeopardised. If you have a weaker connection, like a thin rope, then it may just stretch or even break while having small or no impact on your life. It would have more 'give' in it. But if your connection to it is strong, like a steel chain, then it wouldn't, and that thing could really move you. Any little shift would put you in tension.

A marathon runner might care less about their ability to sing, but if their knee blew out, that could cause them some concern. As we go through our lives, we tether ourselves to various things and people. Different people have different things of importance to them, with varying levels of importance. The more important things are to us, the more we are put in tension when they shift.

The devil wants to find out what things we are tethered to, and use them to put us in tension – like stuff breaking, theft, redundancy, sickness, ruined relationships, etc. These are ways we are put in tension, and they can make us shift our focus, reduce our overlap, and lose our feeling of peace.

How do we avoid tension?

> *For those who live according to the flesh set their minds on the things of the flesh, but those who live according to the Spirit, the things of the Spirit.*
>
> *Romans 8:5*

Those who live according to the Spirit (of which peace is a fruit) choose where to set their minds. There are so many verses we could use here, and all of them would point to the same thing, that we are to keep our minds on the right things and to take captive our thoughts. We need to choose where we put our thinking, imagination, attention, and meditations. We need to focus on making life and peace-giving connections strong, so we don't even have the resource to strengthen ones that don't produce good fruit! Fulfil the desires of the Spirit so you won't fulfil the lusts of the flesh (Galatians 5:16).

The Bible tells us not to worry about the food we will eat or the clothes we may wear. Don't have strong connection to them. You know that your Heavenly Father will sort these things out when you seek first the good things (Matthew 6:33). The more we know our God and are connected to Him, the weaker our connection to other things, and the less they can be used to put us in tension.

This goes for every area of our lives. The more we look to the things of this world instead of to God to give us purpose, value, worth, provision, etc., the more we are connected to them and the more we give them the ability to put us in tension. Our hope (connection to Him) is an anchor to our soul. If we are joined to Him, then stormy seas won't move us.

This is the ideal. He will keep in perfect peace those whose minds are stayed on Him.

If you are reading this and you do not know if you are saved, there is tension in your life that can only be solved by accepting Christ's redemption. There is peace you need to receive that comes only through the Cross, and this gives us right standing with God, being one in spirit with Him.

What things are important to be connected to?

The more time and effort we spend focussed on our relationship with Him, the more we invest in making our connection with Him strong, the less we have available for making strong connections with other things. God is our rock, our anchor, our firm foundation. He will not move and put you in tension, but are you too connected to things that will?

Do not focus all your efforts on trying to break chains in your life. Instead, focus on connecting, remaining, and abiding in Him. The devil will get you all twisted up in chains that will rust, corrode, become brittle, and break, as you press into God. God can and does help us, and we should pray about these things, deny ourselves and crucify our flesh. But our focus on connecting with Him should be greater than our effort to remove chains from our lives. We do not set our minds on the Spirit more by focussing our minds on the flesh more. As Paul says, "Forgetting what is behind, I press on."

Temptations, Trials, and Tests

Are you aware that in order for you to crush the enemy under your feet (Romans 16:20), he needs to get close enough to step on? I had previously assumed that if I encountered a temptation, trial, or test in my life, it was just God carrying out His master plan. But what if you knew the situation being faced had nothing to do with the will of God?

> *Therefore, do not be unwise, but understand what the will of the Lord is.*
>
> *Ephesians 5:17*

I may use this verse a lot, but I really don't want to be found unwise! If His will is knowable as something separate to other wills, and is supposed to be known, then what is it? Should I submit or do I resist? Knowing the difference would have considerable impact on the way I approached it, and a very large influence on its outcome. I believe there are many who are quite reluctant to call something as not of God, and because of this they won't persevere in resisting it when it isn't. We are warned not to call evil good, that we should abhor evil, and that hating evil is the beginning of wisdom. What makes something the will of God?

Did Jesus face temptation? Did He face trials? Did God test Him? That last question should take a bit more thought. Are temptations and tests the same thing? If so, then according to James 1:13, God can't test us. If they are different, then how?

I see temptations, trials, and tests very differently.

Temptations are an opportunity in which a right or wrong decision can be made, and the wrong choice seems attractive in some way.

It is not a sin to be tempted, but it is if we give into it. Jesus was tempted in all points as we are and was without sin. Without a doubt, temptation can be encouraged by the devil, but it can also be just the lusts of your flesh (James 1:14). These are never from God. Scripture says quite explicitly that God does not tempt anyone. Temptations seem to increase in some of the trials that we face, be it a form of distraction or escapism, but are not themselves the trial. If you are being tempted, don't be unwise. Something is happening that is not an act of God, and should be resisted. Full stop!

Trials are when events happen to us which appear to be negative. I say appear, because sometimes God is at work changing things or redirecting us and, sometimes being unaware of what is going on, we call it a trial. God disciplines, prunes, resists, and chastises, but I would argue trials are not actually from God either. If it is not good, how does it come from the hand of the Father? If it is good, then it is not really a trial.

> *Every good gift and every perfect gift is from above, and comes down from the Father of lights, with whom there is no variation or shadow of turning.*
>
> *James 1:16-17*

Do not be deceived. There is no variation, no shadow due to change – no greyness, no lukewarmness, no partiality. Maybe I am trying to deceive you... how would you know? Very simply, my words would not be what God's Word says. Is the Word of God what you are believing? I don't know how to compel people to genuinely question whether their beliefs are right. It took me a brain tumour, and I really hope it takes others less than that. This is life and death!

> *There is a way that seems right to a man, But its end is the way of death.*
>
> *Proverbs 14:12*

That was dramatic, but I mean it.

If you are grieved by trials (1 Peter 1:6) – which I now understand as the devil (or life) making things hard – you can rejoice at the opportunity to test your faith. When you fall into various trials (James 1:2), then test your faith.

Trials have the potential to develop your character, or remain simply as difficulties.

Trials can be used (worked together) by God to bring about good in our life or in the lives of others (Romans 8:28), but will you work with God to make the most of them?

We can give footholds or opportunities to the devil to use to exploit and devour us, but that is our choice, not God punishing us. Don't give place to the devil! Jesus bore the wrath of God for all sins, past, present, and future. Any punishment was dealt with at the Cross. God is not giving us trials, but we can open the door for someone else to. Regardless of whether you think a particular trial is from God, your response to it will change its usefulness in your life.

Tests are activities that we take.

Once again, it really is not important that you believe what I believe, but that you know what you believe – and I pray for you, as I do for myself, that it is the truth.

I used to believe that tests were what God put man through. However, I found only a couple of events in the Bible that could be interpreted as tests. These tests were in the Old Covenant, and it isn't necessarily obvious what their purpose was. If it was important for us to know that God tests us, then why is it not made clear in His Word? Why is it labelled as from God when people can't understand it. Sometimes the enemy devours people simply because he finds a way to.

In Hebrews 12:11, it says that God's discipline may seem unpleasant at times. Let God show you the better way. Sometimes we can be so proud of our way, so wrapped up in our efforts, that it hurts when God points out His way. Remain humble, walk with Him, and lean not on your understanding. The more a man leans on a walking stick, the more impact he feels when it is taken away. Trust in God's

Word, not your understanding. It may seem unpleasant at times, but truth sets you free.

I have found that some changes in my thinking have come with a good dose of godly sorrow. He does not punish us for choosing the wrong way. However, when we realise there was a better way, it can be unpleasant. There's a big difference between saying God made you crash your car/gave you some sickness/or whatever, to teach you something, and admitting you were only leaning on a way that *seemed* right and now need to repent and ask God to lead you in paths of righteousness. It is important to remember James 1:16-17, don't be deceived when it is not God. The Great Commission says to go make disciples and teach them… not break their legs when they do something wrong.

God wants you sanctified in truth, not in surrender. He is not using situations to see if you'll complain less. But if you do fall into trials, He hopes you will test your faith and develop your character.

What is a test then?

In Matthew 4:7, God says to not put Him to the test, and then in Malachi 3:10, He says to test Him. There is a lot of revelation to be gained here, but simply these are two different types of tests: questioning His character versus giving Him opportunity.

God is saying, "Do not question my character, but give Me opportunity."

In Scripture we find many ways to give God opportunity, like:

- Taste and see (Psalms 34:8)
- Test and prove (Romans 12:2)
- Test me in your giving (Malachi 3:10)
- Test your faith (James 1:3)

These are actions we take, not things we are forced to experience. Give God opportunity in your life; put Him to the test. God might possibly do the testing, but it would be rather unexpected if He did.

For the rest of this chapter, I focus on trials in our lives, and our response to them.

Who caused the storm?

It has become so very obvious to me recently (which should have always been the case), just how much God is for me. He wants to strengthen me, develop my character, grow me into a perfect man, make me more like Him, and help me shine His image more brightly. But people tend to think God will put us through trials for our good. They think He puts difficulties in our path to rise above, to be overcomers and be more than conquerors (Romans 8:37), to give us something to have victory over.

Like Job, I thought everything was God's doing, so I would 'put on my sackcloth and ashes' and wait for each storm to pass. I would try to endure things with a smile on my face, hoping not to get in God's way. He was doing something, so in surrender, I would wait for it to be accomplished. But what if the trial was not from God? What if God was wanting us to make use of the devil's attempts to attack us, to resist it, to conquer, and to overcome the attempts to steal, kill and destroy?

Whether you believe God is behind the curtain pulling the strings and causing a particular trial, or that it is separate to His will, our response to it should be the same... to attain victory. God wants us to win. He is a good Father who leads us in triumph (2 Corinthians 2:14). Like when Jesus was asleep on the boat, regardless of who you think was causing the storm, the appropriate response to it was faith. "Peace, be still."

Sometimes Jesus resists the storm for us, but as in this example, He may be questioning our response. If our Father stepped in and resisted for us each and every time, we would never need to exercise any authority and become strong in the power of His might (Luke 10:19, Ephesians 6:10).

God wants the devil resisted one hundred percent, one hundred percent of the time. You were given authority over one hundred percent of the power of the enemy, so even if God did not resist him at all, you still have authority to completely resist Him yourself, but can you? Everything is one hundred percent doable (possible) to them that believe. When the disciples couldn't cast out a devil, Jesus didn't tell them it was not possible but told them how to remedy their unbelief.

Have you resisted until bloodshed?

God is not the one determining your strength. You are responsible to develop your character. The statement 'God is strong when you are weak' is not saying that God will do everything for you. There may be times when He (as Holy

Spirit wills) or an elder does what we are unable to do at the time, but they should be stirring us to faith and good works, helping us renew our minds, growing us into a perfect man, Christ Jesus.

God wants to see you get stronger, not give the enemy more space to make you more surrendered. God has defeated the devil, but He wants you to crush him under your feet. If you really get this, you start to take more joy in trials knowing that through (by) them, partnered with God, they can be worked to develop your character. God is for you and wants you to be more like Him, and there's no doubt He is mightier than the devil.

Imagine how you would face up to a challenge knowing that your Father was there to support you unto victory. You would take the opportunity to win and please Him, to fight the fight and run the race as one who competes for a prize.

Does this change the way you see trials? The devil does not need an invitation to make your life harder; he is already looking for a way in. The devil is not waiting for God's approval to destroy you; he is already going about 'seeking whom he may devour'.

Trials are opportunities to test your faith and develop your character. Will you allow the devil the result he is hoping for? Or will you use his attempts to steal, kill, and destroy to train and bring about the outcome God wants? Don't be found surprised, unprepared, and unaware of his schemes, giving him a foothold in your life.

Some go to the gym to train their physical bodies. Paul says this profits a little, but it is of much more benefit to develop our character and be strong in the Lord (Ephesians 6:10).

It is a challenging picture, but whether he knew it or not, Job was resisting the devil's attempt to make him curse God, and in the end, he received great blessing.

Why is it so ridiculously hard at times?

Resisting a trial may need only ten percent of our ability – which may be a new personal best for us, but it can feel like it takes us one-hundred-and-ten percent. I remember when I was weight training, it felt at times like it took everything I had to lift those weights, yet a few weeks later the same weights seemed almost easy. What changed? I got stronger and learnt better techniques (developed my character).

Trials can constitute almost anything, like being cut off while driving, a tree falling over, work visas delayed, unemployment, poverty, sickness, demonic oppression, etc. I am going to briefly focus on illness, but this can be applied to many of our trials.

Some people will try to lift a hundred kilograms worth of trial and call their failure 'God's will', without attempting to get success with ten-kilogram trials. God says all things are possible to him who believes, but it's much harder to believe (or there is more unbelief) for the big trials when we aren't faithful in believing Him for the small. We *could* believe, but it might take some training to get there. Some people seem to be almost in the grave before they will test their faith. If God told you your ability to lift a hundred kilograms was going to be needed in the future to free someone trapped in a fire, you might start training with smaller weights now.

The Bible says that if anyone is sick to let him call for the elders (experienced), not the newbies. Elders are those who have actioned what they believe, put their faith to the test, persevered, and developed their character. We can get ourselves into a lot of trouble trying to tackle something like a terminal diagnosis without having had victory with an ankle sprain. This is why we are a body of believers. There are people around us who have tested their faith in trials and grown in character, been faithful with the small and been given more. Do you know who these elders are in your life? Are they available to you?

It is better to test your faith when the consequences are smaller and thus develop your character and become stronger. There can be a cost in pressing and reaching for God's prize, but what is the cost if you don't? What price are you willing to pay? Choose to count the cost now (invest) rather than 'borrow' later and risk not having your request processed in time. God is not mocked; whatever you sow, that you will reap. There is seed time and harvest, but many won't plant until they are hungry.

Don't question God's character if you don't reap what you haven't sown

---

Give Him opportunity.

Sickness or Suffering?

When it comes to biblical healing, I feel there is nothing more important to share than these thoughts on James 5:13-15. I have done a lot of pressing in to understanding healing for my own body, and what I believe God highlighted to me made more impact than anything else I had previously heard. But before I get into my main message on this, I feel it is important to raise some points upfront.

One: God is God. He is for us, and can do whatever He wants within the bounds He has put on Himself, e.g. He cannot lie. I don't always understand the way things play out, but I don't interpret who God is by my experience. He is who He says He is, He is in the business of working things for good (merciful and compassionate), and I place my trust in Him (Proverbs 3:5-6).

As in the record of Daniel praying, God sent the answer immediately, not twenty-one days later (Daniel 10:12). Like the story of the persistent widow in the beginning of Luke 18, God avenges speedily, not as our experience says so. Daniel didn't stop praying, and neither do we. We don't keep trying to convince God to send an answer, we thank Him He already has (believe we receive when we ask) and ask Him for help receiving it. There is an enemy, a kingdom of darkness, an adversary who doesn't want you to receive what God has provided. Like Job, don't let the devil use your circumstances to distort your image of God.

Two: We are called to press and reach. I do not claim to apprehend everything, but I am setting my sights above, on the way that God says they should be, not on the way they are presently. There are a lot of statistics out there (things that have been seen, sight) that we could live by. I am not denying they are factual; I am just not letting the past tell me how my future should go.

Three: It is important to mention that it is very clear biblically we should live in health, not move (oscillate) between being sick and being healed. The Word says many things like:

- You are made righteous – no sin, no curse
- Jesus wants you free from the curse, and to receive the blessing of Abraham
- Deuteronomy 28 lists sickness as a curse, not a blessing
- Jesus came that we might have life
- Holy Spirit gives life to our *mortal* bodies
- The Word gives health (life) to all our flesh
- Taking communion in an unworthy manner leads to harm; taking it correctly keeps you healthy
- And many more...

To me, these describe a good connection to the vine (John 15:5). If you are grafted in, then the life you need flows into you from the root, making you a healthy branch and not so susceptible to damage and sickness. However, there is an enemy roaming about looking for a way in.

But what should our mindset be when it comes to healing, returning someone to health?

A healthy branch is harder to break than one not receiving the nutrients it needs. Fixing its connection to the source of its life can revitalise it and restore it to health. However, no amount of provision from the root is going to repair a nearly snapped-off branch, or one not even grafted in. At this point we need something else, some external intervention – a vine dresser.

Wrong believing does not stop you receiving healing through someone else who has faith (believes), but it can stop you coming to them in the first place (Mark 6:5-6).

- A dead person does not believe correctly
- The lame man at the Beautiful Gate didn't
- The person at the Pool of Bethesda didn't

Your own believing can bring needed healing at times (improving your connection), but it might not be as quick as you would like or need. God's intention is that we believe correctly and stay healthy in Him. If your connection to the vine does not exist yet (an unbeliever), then you may need the fruit or signs of someone who is connected. God does not prevent healing to those whose beliefs are not right, but He does want you to believe correctly. We should always be renewing our minds. Receiving healing is not dependent on correct believing, but at times it can help.

It's not about prying healing out of God's hand, but we can team up to get our health back from the one called the thief. Sometimes, our ability to act on our belief (faith) might be all we need ("Your faith has healed you"), and other times we need to join forces.

Lastly, I mention ahead that God has compassion on whomever He wills, and I want to explain what that means to me. Sometimes, there is no natural answer, e.g. people who experienced Jesus coming to them in a vision and healing them, or others feeling that God put it on their heart to pray for someone. Did God work independent of man's prayer, or because of it? I won't be making up some reasoning that suits what I want to say. The Bible is full of things that I don't have an answer for. So rather than make something up, I'll call it God's compassion.

What I do know is that the stuff God wants us to know, is written in the Bible.

Revelation

> *Is anyone among you suffering? Let him pray. Is anyone cheerful? Let him sing psalms. Is anyone among you sick? Let him call for the elders of the church, and let them pray over him, anointing him with oil in the name of the Lord. And the prayer of faith will save the sick, and the Lord will raise him up. And if he has committed sins, he will be forgiven.*
>
> James 5:13-15

Is anyone suffering? Let him talk to God. Is anyone sick? Let him talk to man. Wait, what? Talk to man?

That might seem a very different way to put that verse but imagine with me this was how it was supposed to be understood. How would that affect your pursuit of healing? What if God had nothing at all to do with your receiving or ministering healing, no choosing or deciding, and that it was only a result of your ability, or someone else's, to believe as per Matthew 21:21, Mark 9:23, Mark 11:24, Mark 16:17-18, Luke 8:50, John 14:12, Acts 3:16, James 5:14.

I wanted to challenge this immediately the first time I read it that way.

It made no sense to me God saying, "Don't talk to Me about healing, but get someone else to." So, with a friend I looked at the uses of the word pray. The first two uses of pray from James 5:13-15 are translated the same, i.e. talk to God. The next one, however, 'prayer of faith' is used only three times in Scripture, and two of their uses have been translated as vow.

Read verse 15 again using vow, and see how it reads. Vow of faith – a commitment to act in belief, not the ability to talk with God.

So why pray regarding healing?

Talking to God about healing is not about asking permission, rather it helps us to believe what He says, His report, His yes. It is strengthening our connection to the vine, pressing in to renew our mind, and growing in our understanding of who He is and who we are. Jesus says that if we believe in Him (a position strengthened through prayer), we will do what He does. Read Mark 9:29 again. It says that this type only comes out with prayer, not with granted permission. We need to pray, to talk to God, so we know how to operate in our position as believers, to deliver God's yes.

This sure put a spanner in my thinking. This would mean that we are responsible to believe right, right? Can't we just live our lives however we want and beg God occasionally, when our bodies are less than ideal?

The popularised Christian religion seems so opposite to this today. People will go to pastors, counsellors, psychiatrists, family, friends, anyone with an ear when they suffer (fellow man), and then when doctors say they can't help, they are found begging God in desperation, hoping it is His will to heal them.

I personally don't know many who minister healing today. Why is that? Is God just choosy about who He heals, or am I believing wrong? To be very clear, I am talking about biblical healing (the supernatural kind) for the rest of this chapter, not a physician's ability to treat symptoms.

God is capable of healing anyone He wants, so people tend to think that He decides to heal some and not others, or only some symptoms. Holy Spirit manifests gifts of healing through men as He wills. What on earth makes Him will? I've prayed for a number of people who didn't get healed, and some who did. Did God choose?

This raised some very challenging questions for me personally. It seemed to me that God healed who He chose. I want that for me, and for many others too. What did they have that you or I don't, we might ask? I thought God was good, compassionate, and merciful.

In this mindset, we start to question who God is by how life goes, instead of questioning how life goes by who He is. As the clay, we can start telling the Potter how things should be done (Romans 9:20-21). We determine that God can't have compassion or mercy on whomever He wants, and that He has to have compassion on the ones we want (Romans 9:18).

If it is purely God's choice, then all we can do is ask. If it doesn't happen right away, we may try looking for some other way to twist God's arm, by begging, fasting, bargaining, trying to be more holy, etc. We could even go to yelling and cutting ourselves, like the so-called prophets of Baal on Mount Carmel.

It was rather surprising for me to arrive at the conclusion that there seem to be no God-only healings in the New Testament. They all occurred via a man laying hands, using pieces of a man's clothing, a man's shadow, or a man's command. What I mean is, we have no example of a man in the New Covenant simply talking to God (praying) about needing healing and receiving it. I have no doubt stuff like that happens, but it is not our given example.

This thinking – that we can't ask God for healing – could deflate your hopes of being healed or bringing healing, but the following may bring your hopes higher than they have ever been. I could make up stuff, some reasoning, some tradition to hand on which makes you feel comforted and which makes God's Word of null effect. But I won't be found doing that. I want to know the truth and focus on what is written. So, what is written?

Talk to man

First things first. I am not saying that God can't heal without any apparent involvement from a man. He has compassion on whomever He wants, and we should hope in His mercy, but He would prefer healing came through a believer, be it you or somebody else. I will say that again to be clear: He would prefer healing to be ministered by a believer (rule), but sometimes He is moved with things like compassion (exception).

Secondly, just as God has already provided salvation for all (everyone) through the Cross, He also provided healing for all (every case) when Jesus bore the stripes.

Salvation is already available to all, to whomever, right now. God wants all men saved, and is longsuffering with us, hoping we will take what's on offer (2 Peter 3:9). Whether people receive it or not has nothing to do with its provision.

I never have to beg Him for it. He gave salvation by grace; I receive it by faith.

Healing is just the same. He has already said yes to everyone being healed and chosen. He has made it available, and our part is to say amen (agree, receive it). All the promises in Him are yes and amen. If you are in Him, then imitate those who through faith and patience inherit the promises (Hebrews 6:12).

You wouldn't question the provision of eternal life, so why would you question the provision of healing? Because some people don't receive it?

> ...*Who forgives all your iniquities,*
> *Who heals all your diseases...*
>
> *Psalms 103:3*

One verse with only a comma in the middle – but people use their experience to separate the two. Both are provided. What's easier to say?

What gives me tremendous hope is that I don't in the least bit have to convince God to say yes. He has already said it. I won't be found doing a single thing to try and convince God to provide for me; He's already provided.

I do, however, pray along the lines of the Lord's Prayer... "Give me this day my daily bread; deliver me from the enemy." I thank God He has provided salvation and healing; my prayer is to help me receive and walk in it. I'm not trying to twist God's arm to do His part. I'm giving Him my arm, and saying, "Lead me in paths of righteousness and help me do my part." But enough about me.

Just as Christ is not going back to the Cross every time someone receives salvation, He is not going back to the whipping post every time someone receives healing.

> *But He was wounded for our transgressions,*
> *He was bruised for our iniquities; The*
> *chastisement for our peace was upon Him, And*
> *by His stripes we are healed.*
>
> Isaiah 53:5

There is not a single person deserving of salvation. All have sinned at some point, which means we are all deserving of the wages of death. But God in His mercy sent Christ to die for us while we were yet sinners. Before your body needed healing, Jesus bore the stripes, saying yes for your healing.

You will not convince God to provide healing for you, He's already convinced.

Not what *would*, but what *did* Jesus do?

While Jesus was on the earth in His body, He did His part, which became our example. Christ showed us the reward of what His stripes bought.

> *When evening had come, they brought to Him many who were demon-possessed. And He cast out the spirits with a word, and healed all who were sick, that it might be fulfilled which was spoken by Isaiah the prophet, saying: "He Himself took our infirmities and bore our sicknesses."*
>
> *Matthew 8:16-17*

He did His part, now we must do ours.

Imagine going to the cinema and buying a carton of popcorn to eat while you watched a movie, then sitting down to find only a quarter of the box was full. You would not be impressed to get less than you paid for, especially if people were counting on it. Christ paid so much more than the price of some popcorn. People are counting on it being available. Let's make the most of the price He paid.

The way I think a lot of people have viewed healing is like a slot machine. They pull the lever, they pray once, and see if they hit the jackpot. I don't hear of many people getting healed this way.

The way the Bible talks about healing is more like playing golf, where a healing is the same as getting the ball in the hole. It is possible to get a hole-in-one, even for an absolute beginner, but the more you develop your character, the higher probability you have of that happening.

Can we develop our character?

'*If* we have faith, *if* we can believe, *if* we remain', indicates that we might not. Let's be very clear that the Word is not saying, "If it be God's will," but, if *your* part to play is sufficient, if *your* character has been adequately developed.

Scripture says:

- Be strong (Ephesians 6:10)
- Test your faith and develop your character (James 1:2-3, Romans 5:3-4, 2 Peter 1:5-8)
- Renew your mind, *then*… (Romans 12:2)
- More will be given to those who are faithful in the small (Matthew 25:21)
- The kingdom is like a seed that grows, but only those seeds that are well planted, bring a harvest, some thirty, sixty, a hundred-fold (Matthew 13:8)

In this analogy, be good at golf. If your part is good enough to get the ball in the hole, healing will happen. Vow of faith. Jesus was a pro golfer. Are you taking responsibility for your part?

How many hits will you take?

The surer you are that healing will happen (fully persuaded), and the more important it is to get the ball in the hole, the more hits you will take. If someone said you would get a large sum of money if the ball entered the hole, you wouldn't even count the number of swings to get it in there. You might only pray once for a sore knee, but a few more times if it was a loved one dying of a terminal disease. How important it is to you to get the ball in the hole, will change how much better you want to be (believe, have faith, develop your character) and the more swings you'll take (perseverance).

Like a golfer, generally the more you play the more accurate you get with your shots. The more you choose to test your faith and persevere, the more your character is developed. Run in such a way, according to the rules, that you will obtain the prize. People think they can get away with not playing their whole lives, then have a high probability of getting a hole-in-one because they desperately want it. Although it doesn't happen like that very often, a hole in one is possible whenever you swing.

Without your realising, God might walk on to the green and move your ball to the hole for you, but that is as He wills, and you have no authority to tell Him how to 'spend His money' (Matthew 20:15). The Holy Spirit can be compared with your caddy. He gives you much needed advice on how to take the best swing and which club to use. Sometimes He will tell you what the enemy is trying to hold on to. He at times will give you a special ball that finds its way into the hole, no matter how badly you swing.

What is keeping you off the course?

Elders are not God's chosen gift to mankind, they are like a golfer with a low handicap, simply someone with more experience at getting the ball in the hole. What led them to be on the green is oftentimes suffering. People don't often test their faith, improve their golfing, until facing a trial. Then they pull out their clubs. It isn't important to them to play until it's important to sink a ball.

Consider it pure joy when you have an opportunity to test your faith. When the enemy gives you something that can develop your character, take advantage of it, take it to your coach (pray) to lead you in victory.

You don't have to face hardship personally before you look to develop your golfing game. You may not be called to be on the green full time, as compared with the five-fold ministries, but in Christ you are to know how to get the ball in the hole. You are to grow up into Christ in all things (everything). Don't wait until you have no time to practise. Like a weightlifter, don't wait till you have to lift a hundred kilograms before you choose to train with the tens.

Find someone who will build up your golfing skills, to encourage you to get on the course, to stir you to faith and good works. Take or make opportunities to test your faith. Go pray for people, get on the green, not looking at your past performance to determine how you will play the next round. Press (swing) and reach (aim). You don't know when your golfing (faith) will be called on.

If anyone among you is sick and unable to swing well for themselves, find someone who can, and get that ball in the hole. God has said yes. Give Jesus what he paid for, and get someone on your team (an elder) who has practice saying amen.

Healing Hype

At times I feel quite relieved that I was not responsible for writing the Bible. Some things in there I find challenging to understand. The carnal mind seems to be at enmity with what God says, and I have to accept His Word by faith as true, despite my ability to grasp it. As I write this book, my desire is great to understand biblical healing. I want the truth, whether I comprehend it or find it comfortable. I would love it if I could just say a Christian "Abracadabra!" and see people healed, but that is not found in the Bible.

I want to finish this book by sharing what has led to seeing healing occur in the lives around me. Though there is more to press in to and reach for, I will not let what I don't know stop me from sharing what I believe will lead to the healing of many. God wants you to be in health, and so do I.

There is a great demand for understanding healing, and considerable confusion around it. Many need or want it, or desire to minister it. I used to think, "God, You knew this was going to be the case, so why not make it easier to understand?" Then I stopped looking in the Bible for what I wanted it to say, and started reading to see what it actually said.

Being blunt, Jesus didn't teach on healing, as there is nothing to teach. You either see it as a fruit of believing right, or you don't, in which case, you need to remain in Him and renew your mind. End of story!

But wait there's more

You may be thinking that I am saying you don't believe. This is worth some serious thought. What makes a believer? Regardless of what you think is the biblically correct formula for releasing healing, the Bible says that nothing is impossible to them that believe (Mark 9:23). People have said that they were believing for something, and didn't get it – just like the disciples who despite all the miracles they had seen (Mark 9:19), Jesus still told them to fix their believing. So, if you are not seeing healing, what are you believing?

I previously thought a believer was simply someone who knew they had a spot in heaven, but I discovered this is not the case. You and I can completely misinterpret what the Bible says, live in unbelief or wrong belief, not do what God wants, have only a *form* of godliness – and still inherit salvation. Ponder how many denominations there are due to people not agreeing on what to believe. Some only believe in what *seems* right... but what *is* right?

How many church splits came about because their focus was on right and wrong, not life and peace?

There is big difference between saying the redeemed will lay hands, and believers will. In fact, how many verses promise things to believers? It would seem some believers could impart miracles without knowing Jesus or being redeemed (Matthew 7:21-23, Luke 9:49-50). Despite receiving salvation, we still need to grow in our believing.

I am not questioning whether some people are redeemed or not. I'm challenging what is believed by those who are. The Bible clearly says to renew your mind, i.e. fix your believing, and then you will be able to prove what is His will. Prove here means make it happen, not find out what it is. His will is knowable and supposed to be known. In hoping to avoid any confusion, I am saying plainly that you can be saved by grace, redeemed, and be in a process to believe correctly about other things, e.g. healing.

Paul said he didn't apprehend all, so there is probably more available to us. He hadn't grasped the fullness of why God had laid hold of him for, but pressed on, and said we should, too (Philippians 3:13-15). I don't know why some things have gone the way they did, but I choose to believe God's Word and reach for the way He says things should go. He does not lie.

So how should we believe?

Firstly, and most importantly – there is no way around this – 'Thy word is truth'. It is true regardless of what our carnal brain can reason. There is seemingly no one translation of the Bible that is perfect. Some are pretty good, but even then, they should be compared with others. What should we be exercising? Patience, perseverance, endurance, longsuffering, or steadfastness? Which is a fruit of the Spirit, and which is to be used when testing our faith? In what situations are we supposed to be putting up with things, or instead, fighting the good fight? I believe these differences are a good thing in that they require us to put effort into finding out and to consciously know (choose) what we believe.

The best translations for me are word-for-word ones. I want to know what was said, not just accept someone's opinion. I typically used to read paraphrases, as it took little effort to quote someone else. Now it matters to me that I quote God. Although at times I refer to paraphrases to see what others think, I now primarily read word-for-word versions and ask God what He wants me to hear. God can use anything to speak to you, even a comic book, but there are translations that make it easier for Him to speak through, as they are more in line with what He wants you to hear.

We live by faith (belief in action) and not by sight (experience). The Word is forever settled. Jesus is the same yesterday, today, and forever. God changes not, He is not a man that He should lie. The Word is just as true today as the day it was written/spoken. This means the Bible should be read as though we have experienced nothing. I choose to believe the Bible over my understanding (reasoning). There is absolutely no point in believing anything different. We think we don't understand healing because we let our experiences dictate what to believe.

In finishing on this point, I believe it is crucial to be clear that the way God interacted with people in the Old Covenant, is not the way He interacts with those in the New. God is the same, but his dealings with man have changed.

People use examples from the Old Covenant way God interacted with people, to explain events in their lives today. There is much teaching on trying to make the new wine fit the old wineskin, and vice versa. God can use anything to speak to us, but we cannot mix the two Covenants.

Jesus accomplished a lot for those in the New Covenant. Don't ruin it by trying to live by the Old.

I still read the Old Testament and seek God speaking to me from it, but if I want to see how God interacts with people now, I look at Jesus. In the Old Covenant, you might have been stoned to death. In the New, Jesus says, "Neither do I condemn you; go and sin no more." In the Old was the curse. In the New, Jesus became a curse, and set us free from it.

When I read God's Word, I have already chosen to believe it is truth. All that is left is for me to act on it. Are your actions based on believing right?

Secondly, you must understand that the future can go the way you believe. Otherwise, buckle up and enjoy the ride as best you can. Ultimately, do we believe only some things are possible to them that believe, or all? God lets us choose whether we press and reach to possess (receive) what is provided. God has *plans* for you to walk in, but that is not a promise that you will.

Thirdly, God wants it done. 1 Timothy 2:4 for far too long has been read as, 'God desires that all men receive eternal life'. Not so. It says that He desires all men be *sozo* (saved). It was the faith of the woman with the issue of blood that made her *sozo*. There is *sozo* for your spirit, your soul, and your body. All three of these are *sozo*, but it's only the *sozo* in your spirit that grants you eternal life.

Jesus healed all who came to Him then, and He is the same now. It doesn't matter who you are, God is no respecter of persons; there is no variableness in Him. If you think anyone deserves healing more, or less, than you do, your thinking is wrong. Jesus went about healing all. Jesus said the believer will lay hands – not ask permission. James 5:16-17 says that if anyone is sick, they should go to a believer and get healed.

Once you get a proper grasp on those points, I believe more than half the work is done. The rest is found in how to act.

The Bible says to go make disciples, which means to me go live with people. We don't seem to have many people to imitate when it comes to healing. Paul, when he was on earth, said to imitate him, but since he is no longer on earth, we can only read his letters, not walk with him. Paul said, "I did not come with words, but demonstration." Do you know anyone who is demonstrating, walking in, and receiving the fruit of what they believe? An elder in healing?

I can talk about the way that I walk, but to most of you they are just words. I strongly suggest that you find some people to walk with who also have success. Actively, intentionally, make it your goal to seek these people out. You need to be stirred. You can find people on the internet, but I suggest that trying to catch something from the internet or a book will be much harder than walking with someone. Watching healing testimonies is good for building your faith, but in my experience, these tend to show more what *can* be achieved, rather than how or why.

The things that have led to success in my life are as follows:

Submission

Does God's Word tell you to minister biblical divine healing? If it does, then it is not a choice for you to make, it is an instruction to obey. Regardless of whether you have had the right experience in the past, does not mean you are dismissed from the responsibility of obeying. If you have gotten anxious in the past, this does not free you from pressing into it, fighting the fight, being diligent to enter the rest of believing God, and reaching for it.

Does the Bible tell you to minister healing?

Jesus – our example and who we are to grow up into in all things (Ephesians 4:13-15) – went about doing good and healing all (Acts 10:38). "Just as the Father sent me, so I send you" (John 20:21). He commanded His disciples to go (Matthew 10:5-8), then He told them to teach others to observe (do) all they were commanded (Matthew 28:20). Believers *will* lay hands (Mark 16:16-18). If you believe in Jesus, you *will* do the same works (John 14:12). He gave you authority over all the works of the enemy and told you not to give him a foothold. Are you? Is sickness a work of the devil?

In Acts 10:38, the healing Jesus did, removed the oppression of the devil. It was not stated anywhere in Scripture that He cast God out (not a kingdom divided), or that something was just a result of the fall. He told the bodies of people what to do. He loosed people from evil spirits. He did it that God might be glorified. He did it so that what the prophet Isaiah wrote might be fulfilled (did His part), 'He Himself took our infirmities and bore our sicknesses' (Matthew 8:16-17). Why do people think that some sicknesses are from God? Did Jesus not pay enough for some sins on the Cross? Misinterpretation of Scripture, thinking there is some variableness in God (James 1:16-17)? Trying to mix covenants? Their experience? Just because you might not be able to do it yet, doesn't mean you couldn't, or Jesus wouldn't.

I do not question if it is His will, I submit to what I know is His will. This takes zero experience and a whole lot of obedience. My past does not dictate if I should. His Word does.

Resist

The enemy is roaming about seeking whom he may devour. It is his plan to steal, kill, and destroy; to prosper and prevail. We are to fight the good fight and wrestle (Ephesians 6:12). That sounds like we might, at times, need to do more than just pray once. Regarding healing, we need to stop praying "God, come!" so much, and start praying "Devil, go!" The devil might resist in order to find out whether you believe.

Faith

We are called to live by faith, not just use it when it suits. Live what you believe. People seem not to pray about the small stuff, but then blame God for the big stuff not going the way they like. If you believe…! It is the same regardless of whether it is a sore toe or a broken back. Don't let the perceived consequence (sight) be the deciding factor as to whether you test your faith. Living by faith will strengthen you and develop your character to believe for more.

Hope
Have hope. Know God is merciful and wants to help, etc. God is for you, Holy Spirit helps you, Jesus is interceding for you – but you must act for Holy Spirit to help.

Love
It is an action. You should pray for people because you want to see them set free. Hate sickness. Do not tolerate it. Stop letting the devil have a foothold in people's bodies.

Anointing and authority
If God told you to do it, you are anointed. If that anointing needs power, you need authority. You have been given authority.

Test
Take the test. Test your faith, persevere to victory, and develop your character. When you get victory in smaller things (less consequence), it gives you greater strength to believe for bigger things. Be faithful in the small.

Persevere
We all want God to back up His Word, but will you? It is one thing to know His will, but it is another to submit to it.

Although I don't have a specific chapter on perseverance, much is covered in my writing on authority. I believe one of the leading factors as to why we don't see more healing, is a lack of perseverance. How do you teach this?

Be diligent to enter His rest!

The first verse I used in Chapter 1 of this book is run with 'endurance', or *hypomonē in the Greek*. I write about this word in my previous book, but to me it means persevere. This word is translated so many ways, but they all seem to mean contend.

As per my chapter 'Resist', we need to understand the enemy is no match for a believer who has developed their character – but he sure tries. In many cases, if the enemy resists one prayer, he's won. We are told that when we test our faith to *hypomonē*, it becomes character, and then we will not be unfruitful in our knowledge.

Many will pray (test their faith) but do not *hypomonē*. The healing greats of old are known for what they would do in tent meetings, but do you also know they would travel the world at their own expense to pray for people, move into their houses, set up healing homes, etc. They may have been given to the church, but they also developed their character by learning to *hypomonē*, which is a result of living by faith and not by sight, tasting and seeing, and proving what is God's will. If you learn to do this, you will have so many more victories.

> *Truly the signs of an apostle were accomplished among you with all perseverance, in signs and wonders and mighty deeds.*
>
> 2 Corinthians 12:12

Choice
Pay the cost of taking the test. You might not like what you pay otherwise. The price you choose to pay now, might save you later.

About the Author

Colin is a child of God, a husband to Kelly, and a father to a lovely daughter and three amazing sons. Born, raised and lives in Hamilton, New Zealand, Colin has spent a large portion of his life helping provide worship environments for Believers to enter into. A person who, through his personal trials, has learnt the foolishness of believing man's word in place of God's Word and is now on a mission to point out to all who will listen, what God's Word actually says, and encourage people to believe that. The truth will set you free, but don't take Colin's word for it; take God's.

www.ingramcontent.com/pod-product-compliance
Lightning Source LLC
Chambersburg PA
CBHW051433290426
44109CB00016B/1536